Contents

Project Editor: Larry Olsen
Copy Editor: Bob Wanetick
Designer: Eric Jungerman
Cover Designer: Gary A. Head
Production Coordinator: William Murdock
Illustration Coordinator: Richard Quiñones
Artist: Kelly Solis-Navarro
Compositor: Vera Allen Composition
Printer and Binder: The Maple-Vail Book Manufacturing Group

Library of Congress Cataloging in Publication Data

Russett, Bruce M.
    The prisoners of insecurity.

    Bibliography: p.
    Includes index.
    1. United States—Military policy. 2. Soviet Union—
Military policy.   3. Deterrence (Strategy)   4. Munitions.
5. Arms control.   6. World politics—1945–   I. Title
UA23.R887   1983   355′.0217   82-15981
ISBN 0-7167-1471-X
ISBN 0-7167-1472-8 (pbk.)

Printed in the United States of America

6 7 8 9 0   VB   5 4 3 2 1 0 8 9 8 7

The Prisoners of Insecurity

**NUCLEAR DETERRENCE,
THE ARMS RACE,
AND ARMS CONTROL**

Bruce Russett

Yale University

W. H. Freeman and Company
New York

2

Contemporary Arms and Stable Deterrence

War is not a mere act of policy, but a true political instrument . . . . The political object is the goal, war is the means of reaching it, and means can never be considered in isolation from their purpose.

Karl von Clausewitz

FIRST STRIKE AND SECOND STRIKE

In Soviet–American experiences of the past decades, the stability of deterrence in crisis (no sudden escalation to nuclear war) and the relative stability of the arms race (few very sharp, large increases in spending) both depended on the fact that neither side had a first-strike capability. Existing technology meant that neither side's nuclear retaliatory forces were highly vulnerable. If either side had been highly vulnerable, the situation would have been quite different. It also would have been different if both sides' forces had been vulnerable, that is, if the matter of who struck first could have made a very great difference in the outcome of a war. Knowledge of that could have been highly dangerous in a crisis and also would have fueled the arms race.

The difference between first- and second-strike capability is crucial to understanding both the arms race and deterrence theory. A first-strike capability implies that one could attack and

destroy the other's retaliatory (second-strike) capability and so suffer only minimal damage in return. It could then become very tempting to make the attack. Under conditions of stable deterrence, each side has only a second-strike (retaliatory) capability, not a first-strike force. Each has an assured capability to inflict enormous destruction on an attacker; thus, neither is tempted to attack the other. It is this situation with which most American—and perhaps most Russian—decision makers have become content.

In order to protect their second-strike capabilities, both sides have spent many billions of dollars on research, development, and procurement of advanced weapons. The steps they have taken include:

1. Production of large numbers of delivery vehicles, so that an attacker will not be able to destroy all of them. Both the United States and the Soviet Union have built more than 2000 ICBMs, SLBMs, and bombers.

2. Wide dispersal of delivery vehicles, again to multiply the number of targets an attacker would have to hit and make it impossible for one attacking warhead to wipe out more than one ICBM. Thus, bombers are widely dispersed among many airfields, and ICBM silos are separated. If there is warning of a possible attack, bombers can be further dispersed by having them take off, since planes are much harder to destroy in the air than on the ground.

3. Hardening of the launching sites of delivery vehicles. For example, American missile silos are enclosed in enough steel and concrete to withstand the blast of a near miss.

4. Designing of delivery vehicles for mobility, since a moving target is hard to track and hit. Submarines for launching missiles take advantage of this feature, as would, to a lesser degree, several of the schemes for continually moving around the new American land-based MX ICBM.

5. Concealment of missile-launching sites. Until the era of satellite photography, the United States could not know where most Soviet land-based ICBMs were located. Now concealment has to take other forms. Some of the proposals for mobile basing

of the MX tried to take advantage of this (for example, by putting the missiles in underground tunnels). Submarines, operating hundreds of feet below the surface of the ocean, are well concealed—antisubmarine warfare is not sufficiently advanced to detect them with any reliability. In fact, the submarines for launching American SLBMs (now the Poseidon and the new Trident series of subs) form the most dependable and secure American second-strike force.

Active defense of retaliatory forces is also a possibility. Interceptor aircraft may attack intruding bombers, and a system of antiballistic missiles (ABMs) could, in theory at least, knock down incoming ICBMs. The ABM Treaty of 1972 between the United States and the Soviet Union essentially eliminated this option, the technical feasibility of which was low anyway. Recently, ABM systems (including a possible space-based laser system) have received attention but no advanced development.

Another possibility is to adopt a "launch-on-warning" policy, or, with a verbally more reassuring label, a policy of "launch under attack." By this means, land-based ICBMs that were vulnerable to a first strike would be launched before they could be struck by incoming missiles. This would be desirable only if we could be confident of avoiding false alarms; it might not be desirable even then. We will consider it again later in this discussion.

All these ways to protect nuclear retaliatory forces have required intensive and expensive efforts to provide secure means of command and control from headquarters to the numerous, dispersed, moving, and well-concealed launching sites. The military chiefs must be able to ensure that retaliatory forces would be launched when they were so ordered, that they would be directed to the proper targets, and that they would *not* be launched unless they were given the order. And the civilian leaders—in the United States, the president—must be confident that they have secure command and control facilities in dealing with the military chiefs and that the military people will operate only on orders from the civilian commander-in-chief.

A PRECARIOUS BALANCE?

By the end of the 1970s, a combination of technological change and a change in attitudes made it questionable whether the apparent stability of the arms race achieved in the earlier period would continue to hold. The United States put multiple warheads on most of its missiles and gave them greater accuracy. The Soviet Union continued to build large numbers of land- and sea-based missiles, surpassing the United States. More seriously, the Soviet Union began to deploy a new generation of high-accuracy missiles that were equipped with MIRVs. Since the Soviet rockets had always been substantially larger than their American counterparts, the combination of big missiles able to carry many MIRVs with big multimegaton warheads of great accuracy looked very threatening to some American observers. Specifically, it endangered the ability of even very hardened American land-based missiles to survive a Soviet attack. It became likely that, by the mid 1980s, the American land-based missile forces, composed of Minuteman missiles, would be vulnerable to attack and hence be nearly obsolete as a nuclear deterrent.

A part of the American answer to this danger was to begin to produce MXs, each of which would be bigger than the Minuteman and could have 10 MIRVs instead of the three on the Minuteman rockets. Even if only a few MX missiles should survive a Soviet attack, with their many MIRVs they still could retaliate against enough targets in the USSR to cause "unacceptable" damage. Yet it was by no means clear that even that number of missiles could survive a large-scale Russian attack, especially if the Soviet Union continued to build so many more missiles that they could simply overwhelm the MX force—which might stimulate the United States, in turn, to build more and more MXs. This threatened to turn into a new arms-race spiral, with each side piling on more and more strategic weapons in a futile quest for security.

The MX presents severe problems because of its combination of first-strike capability and vulnerability. The first model of the MX is to have a larger warhead than the Minuteman (335 kilo-

tons instead of 170) and to be accurate within a radius of 600 feet. With these characteristics, each MX warhead would have a 68 percent probability of destroying a Soviet missile silo hardened even to the extreme degree of 3000 psi (pounds per square inch) of blast overpressure. The more advanced version of the MX, due to be deployed in the late 1980s, is to have a warhead of 500 kilotons and an accuracy of 300 feet. Each of these warheads would stand a 99 percent chance of knocking out a silo.

The MX is therefore a "silo buster," a formidable first-strike weapon. If 200 MX missiles should be deployed with a total of 2000 warheads, they would threaten the entire Soviet ICBM force (projected at 1604 in 1986 if SALT II limits are not observed).[1] On the other hand, the MX missiles are themselves vulnerable to a first strike. Whether they were contained in 100, 1000, or 4600 shelters, they could be overwhelmed by those same 1604 Soviet ICBMs armed with MIRVs. Soviet missiles, slightly less accurate but with bigger warheads, would have high "kill probabilities" even against superhardened American silos. Ironically, a land-based MX system would have its best chance to survive if the SALT II limits were observed. Otherwise, the costs to the Soviets of adding another MIRV are roughly comparable to the costs to the Americans of building another decoy (empty) shelter, and there is no apparent cap to the upward spiral of competitive acquisitions.

The alleged risk, therefore, is an open-ended missile race resulting in both sides having forces that could be effective in destroying the other's ICBMs in a first strike. This means, by definition, that neither would have a secure second-strike force. That could be, in the view of some, a very dangerous and unstable situation in a crisis. Many Americans are worried about it.

It could, for example, tempt one or both sides to adopt a policy of launch on warning. That might be all right if we could be confident that the indications of attack were accurate; that is, they were not prone to false alarms and they have complete information and adequate time for reflection and decision. These requirements are severe, given the inevitably short assessment times in the missile age (under 30 minutes from launch to im-

pact) and the tendency of even the best systems to make errors. For example, in 1979 and 1980, three false alarms on the North American Air Defense (NORAD) computer system generated states of alert by American strategic retaliatory forces.

Soviet command, control, and communication and intelligence (known as C³I) facilities are more centralized than those of the United States, but they are also less sophisticated. The Soviet Union may well have adopted a launch-on-warning policy, and that is not comforting.[2] The United States never has adopted such a policy, but neither has it foresworn launch on warning under all circumstances, and there are indications that the Strategic Air Command (SAC) is moving in that direction to protect Minutemen. Perhaps there is no way the United States could convincingly reject the possibility, and maybe it is even desirable to keep some ambiguity: The Soviet leaders could never, therefore, be sure of catching American missiles still on the ground in a first strike. But deliberately to adopt launch on warning, or to encourage the Soviet Union to move toward a more hair-trigger system in order to save their own missiles in a crisis, would be to make the world hostage to human or electronic false alarms.

The arguments favoring large-scale deployment of the MX system assume that current American land-based ICBMs, principally the Minutemen, are vulnerable to a Soviet first strike. With standard information or assumptions about the number, warhead size, and accuracy of Soviet ICBMs, it is easy to reach just that conclusion. But some further assumptions are also required to get support for an assessment of extreme vulnerability. For one, most of the calculations about relative survivability of strategic weapons assume a perfectly coordinated attack, with bombers, ICBMs, and SLBMs all arriving on target at just the right time though launched from many different places at different times. An even stronger assumption is that all the warheads and delivery vehicles are highly reliable—that is, that they will do everything they are technically capable of doing. Both assumptions are, in fact, unrealistic and exaggerate the worst case that might occur for a defender.[3] For example, Soviet missiles typically achieve a reliability of only about 75 percent

even under test-firing conditions; it would be foolhardy for any leader to expect them to do even that well under wartime conditions. Only three American Minutemen have been fired from operational silos since 1965; none worked properly.

Reportedly, "all the problems we know about" have been fixed—but what about those we don't know about? Still other assumptions in computing the missiles' accuracy must be made but cannot be tested. For example, Soviet and American missile tests are conducted at continental latitudes on firing ranges that run more or less on an east–west axis. But in a war between the two nations, the missiles would be fired on a very different trajectory: over the North Pole. For obvious reasons, this has never been done, nor will it be done in peacetime. The editor of *Strategic Review,* a leading conservative journal, indicated the uncertainties this different trajectory introduces. Adjustments for gravity and atmospheric conditions can be tried, but never with complete confidence.[4] Other experts discount this problem. Nonetheless, all these uncertainties should make a prudent decision maker hesitate long before ordering the missiles' use in a surprise attack.

One cannot have this logic both ways. If one argues that the current generation of land-based ICBMs is vulnerable, it is hard to escape the conclusion that a land-based MX will also be vulnerable. By the time an MX system can be deployed, it will be overtaken by the increased number and accuracy of Soviet MIRVed ICBMs. If, on the other hand, one argues that many MX missiles will be capable of surviving a Soviet attack (because of Soviet problems in corrdinating an attack, low reliability of Soviet missiles, or lower-than-expected Soviet accuracy), then the present generation of missiles must be, for now at least, still survivable. Despite all the proposals to move MX missiles around among multiple shelters or base them in superhardened silos, the situation remains basically the same.

Another reason to keep the vulnerability of land-based missiles in perspective is that they are not the only element in American or Soviet strategic forces. Each side also has a large number of bombers able to attack the other's home territory (intercontinental bombers and, in the case of the United States,

American bombers stationed in Europe or on aircraft carriers). Most importantly, each side has many SLBMs on submarines. Altogether, aircraft, land-based missiles, and submarine-based missiles form a triad of weapons. This notion of a triad of different kinds of weapons, each having different capabilities and each protected in different ways, forms a central part of American (and to a lesser extent Russian) strategic planning. Though one or even two parts of the triad might become vulnerable through technological change (as the land-based portion threatens to become), the other elements might still be secure. As long as no major breakthroughs in antisubmarine warfare occurred, those SLBMs could be depended on to create enormous devastation on the other side. As long as they were secure, neither side could really have a complete first-strike capability, and deterrence would remain reasonably stable. In the words of the *Fiscal Year 1981 Department of Defense Report:* "The hypothetical ability of the Soviets to destroy over 90 percent of our ICBM force cannot be equated with any of the following: a disarming first strike; a Soviet advantage that could be made meaningful in an all-out nuclear exchange; a significant contribution to a damage-limiting objective; or an increased probability of a Soviet surprise attack. It would amount to none of these." General John Vessey, Jr., the new Chairman of the Joint Chiefs of Staff, declared, "Overall, would I trade with Marshal Ogarkov? Not on your life."

THE DYNAMIC BALANCE

In Chapter 1 we showed data on American and Soviet capabilities that indicated a continuation of essential equivalence into the mid or late 1980s. Those figures, however, only apply to what is known as the "static" balance of forces: who has what at the beginning of war. With the emphasis in this chapter on vulnerability and the danger of suffering a crippling first strike, the static balance becomes less relevant. What matters more is what is left to the attacked side after its opponent has made a first strike. Will it have enough left to carry out an effective

retaliation? More subtly, will it have an effective choice of targets when forced to fire in a purely retaliatory mode? That is, will it have enough forces to strike at any remaining strategic forces left unfired by the other side and still have anything left after that?

What is imagined here is a scenario in which the Soviet Union attacks American missiles but perhaps spares American cities from a direct initial attack. It then might deliver an ultimatum to Washington: "Quit while you're only somewhat behind. Whatever you do, don't fire at our cities because we have enough missiles in reserve to wipe out your cities in response." Under these conditions, it might make a difference whether the United States had any forces left that were capable of conducting a prompt strike against Soviet silos with any yet-unfired ICMBs.

There is a strong air of unreality to this scenario: It implies that a Soviet leader would have very great confidence in his ability to make a disarming first strike and equally great confidence in the ability—and willingness—of the American President to refrain from hitting back at Soviet cities. Even a limited attack would kill many millions of Americans. The scenario also ignores the fact that there would be many important soft military targets (airfields, transportation centers, supply depots, conventional forces) that American strategic weapons could hit without striking cities. Still, this is the kind of problem that demands attention to the "dynamic" balance of forces, particularly the forces that would be left to both sides after the first exchange of nuclear weapons against each other's strategic forces.

Figure 2-1 shows the changing dynamic balance of strategic forces between the United States and the Soviet Union. The horizontal line across the middle of each graph indicates a position of parity. A line for actual forces above that line indicates an actual United States advantage; below that line, a Soviet advantage. The first graph in each row indicates forces in existence before any use, that is, the static balance. (The first graph in the top row is the same as Figure 1-3.) The next two graphs in each row show conditions after an exchange. The first of these two dynamic-balance graphs shows the relative numbers of warheads available to each side; the second shows their equivalent

32

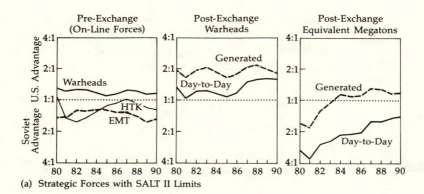

(a) Strategic Forces with SALT II Limits

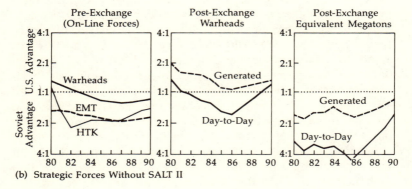

(b) Strategic Forces Without SALT II

Figure 2-1
The Soviet–American strategic balance in the 1980s, including data on the dynamic balance with and without SALT II limitations. [U.S. Department of Defense Authorization for Appropriations for Fiscal Year 1982, *Hearings Before the Committee on Armed Services of the United States Senate*, 97th Congress, 1st Session (Washington, D.C.: U.S. Government Printing Office, 1981), p. 144.]

megatonnage (EMT) taking into account the explosive yield as well as the numbers of warheads. The line labeled *Day-to-Day* represents the pessimistic assumption that the Soviets strike out of the blue, without warning, against an American strategic force

on only normal, day-to-day alert conditions. The dashed line above it represents the more favorable American situation where warning has been received, and some forces have been "generated," i.e., placed on alert (more bombers are ready to fly; most submarines are at sea). Finally, note the line, in the very first graph, labeled *HTK*. This hard-target kill capability, counting accuracy also, gets more nearly to the heart of the "quit while you're only somewhat behind" scenario. (A possibly more relevant measure than this, one where the United States will be behind throughout the 1980s, is called prompt, or time-urgent, hard-target kill capability.)

If the SALT II limitations are observed by both sides (row a), the dynamic balance (after the first exchange of nuclear weapons) will not be too bad for the United States even under the conditions assumed here—those of a Soviet first strike. In numbers of warheads, the United States would retain an advantage whether it was on day-to-day or generated alert status. Its situation would be substantially worse in terms of equivalent megatonnage, at least on day-to-day alert status and on generated alert status before 1983. But again, the bolt-from-the-blue scenario is very unlikely, especially since even then the United States would retain so many warheads. It would hardly be a tempting target for a first strike, except possibly under conditions of great political tension or crisis—conditions when no responsible decision maker would keep American strategic forces on normal day-to-day alert status.

The situation would be considerably more unfavorable, however, if the SALT II limits should be completely scrapped and the Russians were to build their strategic forces up as fast as their physical capabilities might permit (row b). The Strategic Arms Limitation Talks, begun in 1969, led to several important agreements, some of which we shall discuss later. The 1979 treaty, which was never ratified (SALT II), set some limits on the number and kinds of strategic weapons each side might deploy. For example, the treaty called for each side to have a total of no more than 2250 launchers of all types (missiles and bombers) and a ceiling of 1200 on MIRVed missiles (see Figure 2-2). Except for the 2250 limit on all Soviet launchers (they had

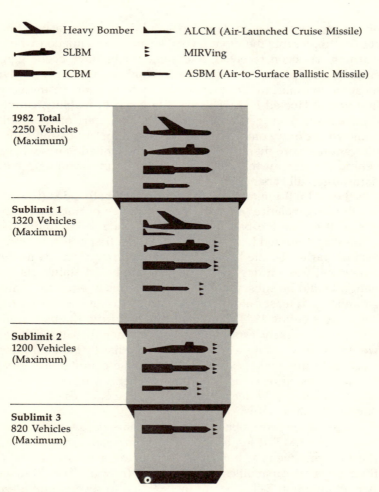

Figure 2-2
Allotment of strategic nuclear delivery vehicles under SALT II. The treaty also provides some restrictions on the deployment of new types of ICBMs, limits on the numbers of MIRVs and air-launched cruise missiles, and provisions for verifying that the agreements have been kept. [U.S. State Department.]

about 250 above that limit at the time the treaty was signed), these limits all were higher than the number of launchers then deployed. Nevertheless, they provided some ceiling to the arms race in terms of quantities (though not necessarily qualities) of weapons. Even though the treaty was not ratified, both President Reagan and Secretary Brezhnev have announced their willingness to obey the agreements if the other side does. Remember also, as we noted in Chapter 1, that the relatively favorable American situation in the mid 1980s is not attributable to the presence of MX missiles. That system could only begin to be deployed at the end of 1986 and could not be completed before the end of the decade.

THE TRIAD

The weapons making up each leg of the triad have different advantages and disadvantages:

Land-based missiles, though the most vulnerable, are the most accurate of the weaponry and can strike their targets quickly. They also are under the most secure command and control and are best suited to those wartime scenarios that imagine some form of "controlled" or "limited" response. In the absence of an effective antiballistic missile (ABM) system (a safe assumption at least for the 1980s), they can be sure of reaching their targets once they are fired.

Bombers also are subject to secure command and control; they can carry very large weapons (bombs of several megatons rather than the up-to-500-kiloton warheads on American MIRVed missiles), and they can deliver them accurately. There is some concern about bombers' continuing ability to penetrate sophisticated Soviet air defenses, but if armed with air-launched missiles (rockets or cruise missiles) the prospects of penetration would remain good. They are vulnerable to attack on the ground, but at least some of them could probably take off in the face of an impending attack. Unlike missiles, they can be recalled if the warning of an attack proves unfounded. They would require

several hours to reach their targets, however, and so are not so useful in a quick attack or retaliation.

SLBMs are the least vulnerable and for this reason have formed an increasingly important component of the American deterrent. They can strike quickly, but problems of launching under the sea (including movement of the submarine and knowing precisely where they are firing from) have until now made them somewhat less accurate than land-based ICBMs. Thus, unlike ICBMs, they do not provide a significant first-strike capability at this time, though this will change later in the decade with the new and highly accurate Trident II system. More seriously, submarines' command and control system is less reliable. Communication with them under wartime conditions is not assured, and their commanders and crews might have to make their own decisions about whether to fire.

The value of the triad, therefore, is not just in covering bets against different kinds of vulnerability, but in different uses of the components as well.

The triad is not a sacred trinity. One or even two of the legs might prove unnecessary for a stable and effective deterrent if another leg could be rebuilt so as to have the valuable characteristics of the leg to be foregone. If, for example, SLBMs could be brought under more secure command and control and their accuracies improved (assuming that high accuracy was desirable), their superiority over land-based ICBMs would be complete. We might, of course, still want to hedge the bet on vulnerability by having another system (such as bombers or cruise missiles) in case the the SLBMs became subject to some technological breakthrough in antisubmarine warfare. But it would be foolish to hedge against vulnerability of what is unanimously considered the *least* vulnerable system (SLBMs) by deploying a new generation of what still is, without serious doubt, the *most* vulnerable type of system (land-based ICBMs). Add to this the fact that multiplying shelters for ICBMs in the United States also means multiplying the number of targets to be hit in the early stages of a nuclear war. Creating thousands of targets that will inevitably, by their number and vulnerability, draw nuclear

fire onto the North American continent would approach the ultimate in organized lunacy.

The Soviet Union actually is much more dependent on the survivability of its land-based ICBMs than is the United States. While the USSR has a triad of sorts, it is very lopsided, with two of its legs extremely short. In 1982 the United States had only about 24 percent of its strategic nuclear weapons on ICBMs; more than half were on SLBMs. The Soviet Union, by contrast, had about three-quarters of its weapons on ICBMs, and heavy bombers carried a mere 5 percent of the total (see Figure 2-3). Even the second-ranking Soviet leg, the SLBM force, is considerably more vulnerable than its American counterpart. Soviet submarines are noisier and less well maintained. Because of the Soviet Union's geographical position (land based with few good ports), its submarines must spend much more time traveling from port to their stations in the deep ocean. More than 60 percent of American missile-launching submarines are on station at any one time, whereas only about 11 percent of Soviet missile-launching submarines are typically on station. All but the new Delta class of Soviet missile submarines must operate in deep-ocean waters if their missiles are to reach the United States. To reach deep water, they must pass through chokepoints—narrow straits such as the Baltic and the Barents seas, the Dardanelles, and the Sea of Okhotsk, off Japan. When coming through these straits, they can be identified by Western forces and tracked thereafter. In addition, American antisubmarine warfare capabilites are much better developed than are the Soviets'. As a result, Soviet SLBMs really are at risk, and an American threat to Soviet ICBMs (such as by the MX) would endanger total Soviet retaliatory capabilities much more than would a comparable Soviet threat to American ICBMs.

POSSIBLE SOLUTIONS TO THE SURVIVABILITY PROBLEM

Several programs have been proposed or undertaken to deal with the threat to the survival of American ICBMs. One, of

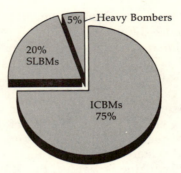

USSR: 8,000 warheads

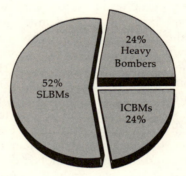

USA: 9,000 warheads

Figure 2-3
Composition of Soviet and American strategic forces, 1982. "Warheads" include individual bombs on bombers.

course—despite its faults and the long time lag until it can be fully deployed—is the MX. Several possible "quick fixes" for the early and mid 1980s include retaining old Polaris submarines scheduled for dismantling and adding new Minutemen silos in which to deploy the 200 Minutemen III missiles now in storage. Both of these, however, would be very marginal improvements: The Polaris subs are armed with the oldest, smallest, un-MIRVed

missiles, and the new Minuteman silos would be just as vulnerable as the old ones. Both could also contravene the SALT II limits and provoke the Soviet Union to exceed its SALT limits if it had not already done so.

Another American program already under way is the building of cruise missiles—essentially unmanned jet-propelled aircraft. More than 2000 cruise missiles are to deployed by mid 1984; they are a major element in American plans to counter the buildup of Soviet MIRVed ICBMs. These will be much cheaper than ballistic missiles and, like airplanes, will travel over land at low altitudes. Equipped with a new kind of guidance system that can "read" the terrain below and compare it with electronic maps, cruise missiles promise to be highly accurate, coming within perhaps 100 feet of a target. Large numbers of these, launched from aircraft or ships, might be able to overwhelm Soviet air defenses and so provide a new kind of strategic weapon. The Americans seem to be well ahead of the Russians in developing this technology, yet it promises to be something of a mixed blessing. Might it not simply fuel a new round of acquisition and counteracquisition in the arms race? It will impose new problems on both sides' information-gathering abilities. Can each reliably count the number of cruise missiles its opponent possessed? And will this new weapon be so accurate and dependable as to become a new kind of first-strike weapon? Probably not. They are much slower than ICBMs and hence give more warning time.

Officials in the Reagan administration reportedly favor a basing plan known as the "dense pack"—putting many MX launching sites within a small area instead of spreading them out. The goal is to take advantage of a phenomenon known as "fractricide," whereby the explosion of one warhead prevents other closely following warheads in the vicinity from exploding. This might prevent or at least delay the destruction of a large number of MX missiles in strongly hardened silos. The technical feasibility of this plan still is in question. Probably it could be reliable only if the missiles in the dense pack also were defended by a new antiballistic missile (ABM) system.

At this time, the ABM Treaty of 1972 limits each side to a single ABM deployment site under rather carefully specified conditions. Both countries continue to pursue research and development, and several technologies offer the chance of some deployment by the end of the 1980s. It is not clear how much could be deployed without violating the ABM Treaty or at least requiring the treaty to be renegotiated. The value of the new ABM technologies is unknown, and there is no way to be sure they would be effective. They could be overwhelmed in a large-scale attack and their radar blacked out. We might easily find ourselves losing the ABM Treaty, which is arguably the most successful piece of negotiated arms control in the history of Soviet–American relations, and embarking on a new dimension of a competitive arms race with no foreseeable gain. The next century holds out the possibility of exotic systems, such as high-energy lasers based on satellites in space. But that does not solve the immediate problem of American ICBM vulnerability (to the extent that it is a real problem), and it raises the same questions about whether an extension of the arms race into the dimension of space-based ABMs is really in America's interest (or the world's).

The other option receiving substantial attention is a proposal to build a fleet of small submarines, each carrying perhaps two SLBMs, to operate within 500 miles of the coast of North America. By being smaller (and therefore quieter) than the big-fleet submarines, they would be harder to detect and could more easily be protected in American coastal waters. Since the ability of the submarines to survive would not be in question, there would be no need to build extras—as with the MX—to make up for those that might be knocked out in a first strike. If 50 such submarines were kept at sea at all times, they could provide enough missiles (100) to serve as a potent retaliatory force without being enough to pose a first-strike threat to the whole Soviet ICBM force. Command and control might be assured by a combination of coastal transmitters (perhaps mobile ones so they could not be easily attacked) and a satellite communication system (NAVSTAR, though it might in turn be vulnerable to Soviet satellite killers). These guidance systems might also make the

small-sub-launched missiles about as accurate as land-based missiles. Several aspects of this system are still experimental, and its probable cost is a matter of controversy. But if it worked, it would avoid the vulnerability problems associated with land-based missiles. Moreover, it would not entail the MX's massive environmental costs nor draw fire onto American territory in the event of war. On these grounds, the small-submarine system is worth very serious consideration. Possibly its biggest drawback is institutional: It would produce a new triad—small subs, big subs, and bombers—that would put the Air Force out of the strategic missile business. We could expect vigorous resistance by those with careers, skills, and sales at stake.

EXTENDED DETERRENCE

To some observers, the major virtue of the MX is just exactly what we have identified here as a vice—its utility as a silo buster in a first strike. Some strategic analysts want to see the United States have such a force. They worry about the problem of "extended deterrence," or the ability of the United States to deter not just a Soviet attack on the United States but Soviet aggression against American allies and vital interests abroad. Some people in Washington have a nostalgia for the early days of the cold war, when the United States had strategic predominance, and nuclear massive retaliation was a plausible strategic posture. Since the Soviet Union lacked the ability to do serious damage to the American homeland, Washington could plausibly threaten to unleash a nuclear strike against the USSR in response to even a conventional Soviet attack on Europe, for instance. In 1962, the United States had conventional air, naval, and military superiority in the Caribbean and a strategic superiority in missiles of 10 to 1. Those forces made American threats during the Cuban missile crisis credible.

Threats like that are no longer nearly as credible. If the United States were to escalate a conventional war in Europe to the nuclear level (even "only" to the extent of using tactical nuclear weapons on the battlefield), it would risk further escalation that

might result in American cities being devastated. In order to be able to enforce one's will in a crisis, so the argument goes, one must be able to dominate the military situation at every level of escalation. If we had such dominance, or superiority, the Soviet Union would have to give in and would not dare to escalate or threaten to escalate to a higher level of force, where it would still be overmatched.

By this reasoning, the United States should have the ability to attack Soviet missile silos and other strategic nuclear installations if necessary, thereby sharply limiting the damage the Soviets could inflict on America in retaliation. If we could make this threat credible, then perhaps the Soviet Union would be deterred from initiating even lower levels of violence—conventional or tactical nuclear—that might provoke an American strategic first strike. In other words, America needs a first-strike force of silo busters, not for aggressive purposes but to defend its allies. Relying on this kind of reasoning, American leaders never have been willing to foreswear the first use of nuclear weapons. Indeed, possible first use of nuclear weapons in Europe has been NATO policy for decades. The United States has long had nuclear weapons in Korea, and their possible first use in case of invasion was affirmed by former Defense Secretary Schlesinger on an official visit to Korea. Possible first use in the Persian Gulf area was declared by President Carter, and an American strategic-weapons alert was part of the implicit bargaining with the Soviet Union during the 1973 Arab–Israeli War.

Whatever the abstract logic of dominating the military situation at every level of escalation, the hope for it defies the facts. Pursuit of a first-strike capability is, in the circumstances of the 1980s, a fantasy. The Soviet Union has essentially caught up with the United States in most aspects of the strategic nuclear balance and is in some respects superior. With over 8000 Soviet warheads now in existence, recovery of anything like a 10-to-1 American superiority is unimaginable. Soviet leaders built to their status of equivalence with great effort and sacrifice. Despite their country's economic problems (and they are severe, though maybe no more so than those of the United States), they can continue to match American efforts. Soviet technology and

economic resources surely are sufficient for the effort. They do not have to surrender equivalence—and will not.

It is not clear how important nuclear deterrence has really been in determining the outcome of past military and political confrontations. A study commissioned by the Defense Department concluded "Our data do not support a hypothesis that the strategic weapons balance between the United States and the USSR influences outcomes. No support was found for the thesis that positive outcomes would occur more often when the United States had the advantage over the Soviet Union in ratios of delivery vehicles and numbers of warheads."[5] It was not Soviet nuclear capabilities (which were nonexistent) that deterred the United States from lifting the siege of Berlin in 1948 by military means or from carrying the Korean War into China in 1951. Nor was it Chinese nuclear forces (which were miniscule) that deterred the Soviet Union from escalating the Ussuri River battle with China in 1969. In each case, the practical deterrent was the prospect of an extended and costly conventional war.

Any effort to establish American strategic dominance means not just an ability to eliminate Soviet retaliatory forces in a bolt-from-the-blue strike. No responsible official seriously contemplates making such an attack. Extended deterrence with escalation dominance would require an even *stronger* capability, one able to eliminate major retaliation if the American first strike were made during a political crisis against *already alerted* Soviet strategic forces. This implies a much greater American superiority—one able to prevail against Soviet forces on generated, rather than day-to-day, alert status. It implies a capability beyond anything the United States has had for almost two decades. It is not achievable and probably not even desirable. If we had it, crises could well become even more dangerous, with each side tempted to preempt before its vulnerable strategic forces could be wiped out by the other's preemption!

Fears about the vulnerability of existing strategic retaliatory forces may well be exaggerated. Talk about trying to build forces that would make Soviet retaliatory forces vulnerable is irresponsible. Notions of combining Soviet vulnerability with the waging of "limited" or "controlled" nuclear war are dangerous.

They may become driving rationalizations for buying and building new kinds of weapons, but they do not contribute to American security. Rather, they risk exposing us to the worst of insecurities.

An unreinforced brick house 4700 feet from ground zero before and after a nuclear explosion at the Nevada test site. The explosion generated 5 pounds per square inch of overpressure, equivalent to 4.3 miles distance from a one-megaton explosion. (Courtesy of U.S. Federal Emergency Management Agency.)

3

What's Wrong with Arms Races?

And let me speak to th' yet unknowing world
How these things came about. So shall you hear
Of carnal, bloody, and unnatural acts,
Of accidental judgments, casual slaughters,
Of deaths put on by cunning and forced cause,
And, in this upshot, purposes mistook
Fall'n on th' inventors' heads. . . .

Horatio, speaking at the conclusion of *Hamlet*

Why should we care about arms races at all? Are they really so bad? After all, nation–states are faced with a security dilemma in this anarchic world of each state against all. Perhaps the continuing, competitive drive for weapons may be the only way to find any security. Arms purchases might therefore provide a necessary and otherwise unobtainable deterrent.

The case against large-scale arms acquisitions rests on three assertions:

1. It is wasteful, imposing an enormous financial burden and squandering resources.

2. It ensures that, if war ever does occur, it will be much more destructive than if such great accumulations of killing power had not been built up. Conceivably, such a war would mean the end of humanity.

3. The continued accumulation of weapons increases the likelihood of major war, especially by increasing international tensions. Arms races are a cause of war.

We shall examine each of these assertions in turn.

WASTE

The amount of money the world spends on military purposes
in one year alone now exceeds the value of the entire output of
the world in 1900 (measured in constant dollars—that is, not
counting the effects of inflation). In 1913, immediately before
World War I, roughly 3 to 3½ percent of total world output was
devoted to the military; now the proportion is about double
that, or between 6 and 7 percent of the world output (gross
national product of all countries). Current world military expenditure equals the value of the gross national product (GNP)
of all Latin American and African countries combined, or total
worldwide government expenditure on education, or the total
income of the poor countries that account for more than half of
the world's population. President Carter, in his October 1977
address to the United Nations, noted that "worldwide military
expenditures are now in the neighborhood of $300 billion a year.
[In 1976] the nations of the world spent more than 60 times as
much equipping each soldier as we did educating each child."
   The two superpowers, the United States and the Soviet Union,
account for by far the largest proportion of this expenditure
(roughly 30 percent each). However, the fastest militarizing area
of the world is the Third World—especially the Middle East,
where, measured in constant dollars, military expenditures have
gone up by almost 17 percent annually since 1955. What this
means in terms of world opportunities foregone—in terms of
misery, ignorance, starvation, and disease left unchanged—cannot be measured precisely, but it can be imagined. As United
States general and Republican President Dwight Eisenhower said,
"Every gun that is made, every warship launched, every rocket
fired signifies, in the final sense, a theft from those who hunger

and are not fed, those who are cold and are not clothed. This world in arms is not spending money alone. It is spending the sweat of its laborers, the genius of its scientists, the hopes of its children."

Investment and Economic Growth

Many people have powerfully argued that military spending drains the economy of productive potential, that by diverting funds and skilled manpower to the dead end of the military establishment, investment and technological innovation in civilian sectors are lost. Defense industries, working under cost-plus contracts with the Pentagon, can afford to pay whatever salaries are needed to attract skilled workers. Normal civilian industries' products must compete in the market with other domestic and foreign goods; therefore those industries have to worry about their costs and the prices they can get for their products. As a result, they often cannot pay the high salaries offered by the defense sector. Either they risk pricing themselves out of the market, or they simply fail to hire enough high-quality labor. As a result, high-technology enterprises and top-flight scientists who might otherwise produce goods and services that could be sold abroad to compete with Japanese and German industry never get to produce those goods.

In the long run, the problems of universities are as serious. Currently, for instance, there is an extreme shortage of Ph.D.s in computer science, and universities cannot even remotely match the salaries offered in the defense industry. Without computer science Ph.D.s to train new computer scientists, the supply of skilled personnel may never catch up to the need. In effect, the defense industry risks eating the "seed corn" (the productivity of future generations) necessary for both its own long-term survival and the competitiveness of high-technology American industry.

It is easy to point to the much lower military expenditures of Germany and Japan (3.2 and 0.9 percent, respectively, in 1979) than the United States (5.2 percent) and their substantially higher growth rates over a long time period. Since World War II, the

United States has carried a substantially higher military burden (military spending as a percentage of GNP) than any other industrialized capitalist country. Such a long-term absorption of high-technology resources for what are economically unproductive uses must have bad effects. Arthur Burns, Chairman of the Council of Economic Advisers under President Eisenhower, put it this way: "The real cost of the defense sector consists, therefore, not only of the civilian goods and services that are currently foregone on its account; it includes also an element of growth that could have been achieved through larger investment in human or business capital."[1] Systematic evidence for this argument, though fragmentary, tends to support it. For example, two related studies report, in a complex analysis of 15 industrialized economies from 1960 to 1970, that countries with higher levels of military expenditure usually had less investment and a lower rate of growth in GNP.[2]

Of course, there is no guarantee that a cut in military spending would result in more investment or in satisfying basic human needs. We do know, however, that the savings from lower military spending in the United States would not all be consumed as beer and swimming pools. From 1939 to 1968, changes in private investment were especially closely related to changes in military spending. On the average, a $1 increase in military spending was matched by a 29-cent drop in investment. Proportionately, that was about three times the amount that consumption fell when military spending rose.[3] In periods of high unemployment and low inflation, this might not be the case; under those conditions, military spending might stimulate the economy, in the longer run producing greater private and public investment. But those conditions have not been seen very often in recent decades. Under circumstances of "stagflation" (economic stagnation and moderately high unemployment combined with high inflation), governments hesitate to stimulate the economy further; military spending is not a bonus but rather has to come at the expense of other things. Investment lost today means a smaller, less productive economy in the future (and, incidentally, a smaller economic base from which to make future military expenditures).

Tradeoffs exist both between government and private spending (consumption and investment) and between different kinds of government expenditure. There may also be tradeoffs within the federal budget between military spending and important civilian programs. It is impossible to find any regular pattern of tradeoffs within the federal budget over the entire 1940–1979 period. This is because in many years there was enough slack in the economy to permit increases in both military and civil government spending (such as in the first years of World War II). In other years, if the economy cannot grow enough, the government may decide instead to maintain a high level of government spending and force cuts in private spending to compensate for it. This may be done either by raising taxes or by running a budget deficit that uses inflation to cut into private use of resources. The former method was used during some of the Truman Korean War years, while the latter was typical of how the Johnson administration financed the Vietnam War. From 1940 to 1979, the typical pattern was for federal spending on health and education to go up at the same time that military spending was rising. This happened in 21 of the 39 years, and in only 2 years did health or education spending go down when military spending rose. (The rest of the time all fell together, or health and education rose when defense cuts provided the opportunity.) The patterns tended to be the same under Republican presidents as under Democratic ones.[4]

By this standard, the priorities of the current administration are strikingly different. President Reagan has acted to raise military spending by very large amounts and to cut many civilian programs by as much or even more. Health and education programs were especially heavily hit in the proposed fiscal 1982 budget, being reduced by approximately 11 and 27 percent, respectively, in real (inflation-adjusted) dollars, while military spending rose by 7 percent. No law of economics or politics required that tradeoff, as shown by the rarity of it in the preceding four decades. Rather, it was a deliberate choice by the Reagan administration and Congress to reduce the total role of the government in the economy while raising the level of military preparedness. If the long-run effect is to spur private in-

vestment, it will enlarge the economic base (including the military potential) of the economy.

The cuts in health and education spending may, however, have very bad effects on national well-being and national strength. National security is more than purely a military matter. National security benefits from a healthy and well-educated population. Even in a military sense, security requires healthy, skilled, and well-trained individuals to serve in the armed forces and work for the defense industries. On the basis of that principle, President Eisenhower sponsored the National Defense Education Act in 1958. On that very principle, too, present policies risk eating up the seed corn for a momentary spurt in military spending.

Employment

Sometimes, military spending is justified as a means to create employment—people can be put to work building weapons or serving in the armed forces. This happened in 1940 and 1941, when the United States began to arm for World War II and, in the process, completed its recovery from the Great Depression. People and factories that would otherwise have been idle were put to work. But that was an exceptional time: The government was willing to engage in deficit spending in order to rearm; it was much less willing to do so for obvious civilian make-work projects or even for large-scale expenditures on behalf of civilian well-being.

Since that time, however, the situation has rarely been so simple. At present, for example, many people are out of work, but the country is also plagued by inflation. Deficit spending may help create employment opportunities, but it also fuels inflation. The government has tried to narrow the deficit in the federal budget and have massive tax cuts at the same time. Under these circumstances, the military increase comes at the expense of government spending for civilian purposes, and military spending reshuffles jobs rather than creates them. Some workers (such as engineers and draftsmen), industries (for instance, aerospace, munitions, and shipbuilding) and parts of the

country (especially the sunbelt) gain jobs; others (unskilled workers, home construction, the Midwest) lose jobs.

Because of the types of jobs gained and lost, military spending actually produces a net *loss* of jobs when it substitutes for civilian expenditures. Military purchases mostly go for high-technology goods made by highly skilled and highly paid workers. The salaries are higher, but the number of jobs is smaller. Careful studies have demonstrated that almost any other kind of spending, either private or public, would create more jobs. The assumptions and methods of these various studies differ, so the details of their results differ, too (see Table 3-1). But the same basic conclusion is common to all of them: Military spending produces fewer jobs than does virtually any other kind of spending, private or public (except for the space program). In short, when military spending is boosted at the expense of civilian spending, the net result is fewer jobs, not more. Another kind of waste, therefore, can be measured in human productivity and self-respect.

DESTRUCTIVE POTENTIAL

Waste is not the worst of sins. We might tolerate it if the arms race did not threaten our very existence.

However, the destructive potential of modern weapons needs little emphasis. Before World War II, military aircraft had a combat radius of but a few hundred miles and could carry only a ton or so of high-explosive bombs. But now bombers and missiles reach halfway around the globe, carrying payloads whose explosive power can be nearly 100 million times that of a pre–World War II bomber. In early 1982 the Soviet Union had 308 SS-18 missiles, each with 10- to 20-megaton warheads. A bomb of that size could destroy most of even the largest city, leveling buildings 10 miles in all directions from the point of explosion. Warheads of only one megaton each (the Soviet Union had at least 6000 warheads of about that size) could level cities of up to 4 miles in radius.

Table 3-1
Four Estimates of Employment-Creating Effects of Defense and Other Expenditures

1. Number of jobs created by alternative expenditures as compared with spending on the B-1 bomber, 1977:

Tax cut	+10,000
Housing	+30,000
Welfare–Public works	+20,000

2. Number of jobs created or lost by changes in defense budget of 30 percent, compensated by opposite equal change in education, health, public assistance, and environmental programs, 1980:

Defense increase	−1,300,000
Defense decrease	+2,000,000

3. Number of jobs created by $1 billion spent for various purposes, 1977:

Defense	45,800
Civilian production	53,000
Antirecession aid to state and local governments	71,000
Public service employment	98,000

4. Number of jobs created by $1 billion spent for various purposes, 1974:

Defense (military personnel)	58,000
Firemen	70,000
Policemen	73,000
Nurses	85,000
Teachers	76,000
Job Corps	145,000

Source: 1. Chase Econometric Associates, *Economic Impact of the B-1 Program on the U.S. Economy and Comparative Case Studies* (Cynwyd, Pa.: Chase Econometric Associates, 1975), table 14, T2.
2. Roger Bezdek, "The 1980 Economic Impact—Regional and Occupational—of Compensated Shifts in Defense Spending," *Journal of Regional Science*, 15, 2 (1975): 183–197.
3. "The Pentagon as Job Creator," *The Defense Monitor*, 6, 7 (September–October 1977): 3.
4. Marion Anderson, *The Empty Pork Barrel* (Lansing, Mich.: Public Interest Research Group in Michigan, 1978), p. 1.

A large or full-scale Soviet attack on the United States, using thousands of warheads to attack urban–industrial targets, would

be devastating. Various studies by the Department of Defense, the Defense Civil Preparedness Agency, and the U.S. Arms Control and Disarmament Agency produce some spread in the estimates of prompt casualties (those occurring within the first 30 days of the attack), depending upon different assumptions about the use of immediately available fallout shelters, wind and weather conditions, and the nature of the blasts (air burst or surface burst). But all the estimates are high, ranging from a top of from 155 million to 165 million (75 percent of the American population) to a low of from 76 million to 85 million. If time were available to evacuate the urban population before the attack, the prompt *fatalities* might still be 20 million to 55 million. While these estimates were made for a Soviet first strike, the assured destruction retaliatory capability of the USSR could produce very nearly the same number of deaths in a retaliatory strike.[5]

Even restricted counterforce attacks would still produce very heavy casualties because of the large number of targets that would have to be hit. An attack only on the existing 1052 ICBM silos, 46 Strategic Air Command bases, and two bases for missile-launching submarines would result in 7 million to 15 million prompt deaths and as many wounded. The Carter plan for basing the MX (now fortunately abandoned) would have raised the number of aim points (and hence targets) to about 5000, counting all the MX shelters which might or might not actually contain missiles, and the existing Minuteman silos. An attack on those targets could have produced between 25 million and 50 million casualties.

The ratio of killed to wounded may in fact be underestimated, because it does not take into account the elimination of medical facilities essential to survival of the seriously or moderately injured. If only one city were hit, patients could be shipped to nearby areas, and doctors could come in from nearby. If all major cities are hit, there would not be much "outside" from which help could come. Take, for instance, the effect of an attack on the 71 largest urban areas in the United States. About 55 percent of the American people live there, but those same areas contain 70 percent of all American physicians. The ratio of still-

living casualties to surviving physicians would at first be around 1000 to 1, dropping as more people died. This compares with an average daily patient load for each doctor of, at most, 25 to 1. Casualties could exceed available hospital beds by 30 or 40 to 1. Most patients would suffer the type of terrible burns that normally are treated in burn-care centers. Only about 100 hospitals in the country have facilities for intensive care of burn victims. One of the best and largest is Massachusetts General Hospital in Boston: Its intensive burn-care unit has 15 beds.

These first fatality estimates are just for the short term, preceding "the worst epidemic that could ever be"; the longer-term effects of losing medical personnel and facilities would be almost as bad as the short-term effects. Critical damage to the economy and society would soon appear. Those same 71 biggest urban areas with 55 percent of the population contain 60 percent of American industry. If, in addition to hitting the 71 urban areas, a "mere" 200 hundred-kiloton warheads were used against the centers of three remaining industries—iron and steel, other metals, and petroleum refining—only 2 percent of the entire national capacity in those industries would survive. Foreign petroleum—if available—could not be landed because the ports would be destroyed. Gas pipelines, oil pipelines, and electricity grids would be fragmented. Without fuel, the entire American transportation system would be crippled. Railroad lines would be chopped up. Water supply and sewage facilities would break down all over, creating epidemics and further straining the already impossibly overburdened doctors and hospitals. Antibiotics and other medical supplies would be quickly exhausted. Radiation damage would lower people's resistance to disease. If food were still available in the agricultural areas, it could not be processed and shipped, since those facilities generally are in the metropolitan areas. Food would rot on the farm while remaining supermarket shelves, which normally contain only a week or two of stocks, would be immediately emptied. Starvation would be widespread. (In government civil defense plans, people evacuated from the cities are told to bring their own food!) Many people would be in extreme psychological shock, unable to work effectively.[6]

Things hardly look better in the still-longer run. Much farmland would be made radioactive. The centers of finance and government would be destroyed, producing political and economic chaos. The highly interdependent industrial society in which we live would be completely fractured. Many of the nation's centers of higher education (people, buildings, libraries, computers) would have vanished (72 percent of the country's professional students study in those 71 urban areas). Imagine a situation where the federal government (Washington, D.C.), the Mayo Clinic, Wall Street, the Omaha stockyards, the Massachusetts Institute of Technology, and most of the secondary and tertiary centers like them had been wiped off the earth. What remains is the kind of society that would have to reconstitute itself and recover. A few federal officials have fantasized about shelters and evacuation plans. Thomas K. Jones, a deputy under-secretary of defense, reassured us: "Everyone's going to make it if there are enough shovels to go around." He might rather say that in the postwar environment, shovels would be about the only things that would work.

No possible level of preparation or civil defense can mitigate this disaster very much. Some people worry that the Soviet Union, which has undertaken an extensive civil defense program, could shelter enough of its people to come out of the war in some recognizably winning posture. That fear is not realistic. By one estimate, a full-scale U.S. retaliatory strike against Soviet industry and military centers would leave 100 million dead immediately if there were no civil defense, 25 million to 35 million dead if the cities were evacuated, and 70 million to 85 million dead if, after evacuation, the United States aimed at the evacuation sites. By another estimate, likely Soviet casualties would amount to 55 million people despite civil defense.

According to the CIA, "Under the most favorable conditions for the USSR, including a week or more to complete urban evacuation and then to protect the evacuated population, Soviet civil defenses could reduce casualties to the low tens of millions."[8] The Office of Technology Assessment states that "U.S. retaliatory attack against the Soviet Union would destroy 70 to 80 percent of its economic worth. . . . The effects of a large-scale

nuclear attack against Soviet military and urban–industrial targets would remove that nation from a position of power and influence for the remainder of this century."[9]

We have not even mentioned long-term ecological results, such as depletion of the ozone, global weather changes (which would affect crop-growing seasons), selective destruction of some plants and animals and the survival of the hardier forms, cancer from radioactive fallout, etc., etc., etc. One author refers to survivors as a "republic of insects and grass" and raises the prospect of the extinction of mankind.[10] Some critics believe the danger is exaggerated—that while civilization might be destroyed, humans would continue to exist even after an all-out conflagration.

Is it really better to contemplate only the end of civilization and not the end of the species? Maybe we can console ourselves that civilization would survive, somehow and somewhere. Maybe—but again, at what level of living, culture, and sophistication? Conditions would be harsh, in ways that are now hard to imagine and that go well beyond the basic images of destroyed capital, fragmented societies, and radioactive surroundings. Here is one example, drawn from the work of Harrison Brown:

> A part of the tragedy is that once industrial civilization disappears it will probably not return to the earth for an extremely long time— if ever. Industrial society was able to grow as rapidly as it did in part because of the ready availability of high-grade mineral resources including fuels. As time passed and demands rose, the grades of ores gradually decreased. . . . The time must inevitably come when ores as such no longer exist and industrial civilization will feed on the leanest of earth substances—the rocks which make up the surface of our planet, the waters of the seas, the gasses of the atmosphere, and sunlight. The technology required to carry out processing will become increasingly complex. Nevertheless, as long as the technology is functioning smoothly, industrial civilization can continue to thrive. But should industrial civilization perish, it is difficult to see how it can get started again.[11]

Although we are not yet at the point of using "the leanest of earth substances," for some materials we are surprisingly close.

In an earlier book, Brown and his coauthors pointed out that the Bronze Age simply could not be repeated on this earth. Bronze Age people fashioned their tools easily from crystals of very high-grade ore on the surface of the ground. Those ores have long since been exhausted; for instance, commercial copper smelting now works with ores containing only about 0.6 percent copper, requiring an extensive—and expensive—technology.[12] Not only can the material base to support advanced technology be lost, the technology itself may be lost. Brown gives us an example:

> With the decline of Rome, Nero's circus fell into disuse and in time an extremely large obelisk in the center of the track fell over, where it remained prone for eleven centuries. In the sixteenth century Pope Sixtus V developed a plan to erect the giant stone in front of the Basilica of St. Peter in the Vatican. To move so huge a mass using Renaissance technology was so complex an undertaking that all mathematicians of Christendom were asked to submit proposals. One plan was selected out of fifty suggestions and on April 30, 1586, after many difficulties, the obelisk was finally lifted, placed on rollers, and hauled to the center of the square to the sound of all the Eternal City's church bells. In September the stone was pulled upright to the cheers of a huge crowd.
>
> This considerable engineering achievement was hailed in song and story. Paintings and poems glorified the event. But few people at the time appreciated that the Romans over twelve centuries earlier had floated the huge pillar down the Nile from Heliopolis to Alexandria, then transported it by ship to the Tiber, then transported it several kilometers overland to Nero's circus, now the site of the Vatican, where they erected it. Further, this was but one of dozens of such objects which the Romans had brought from Egypt and erected in various parts of the city, largely for decorative purposes. With the decline of Rome, the engineering and organizational skills which enabled the Romans to accomplish such gigantic tasks with such apparent ease were lost.[13]

If the arms race had been halted two or three decades ago, civilization-threatening levels of nuclear destruction would not have been attained. But it wasn't, and they have. The longer

the race continues, the potential destruction—and the threat—
will become still greater.

LIKELIHOOD OF WAR

If we could be sure these destructive capabilities really would
never be used—that the "balance of terror" would be reliably
stable—they might be tolerable. But there can be no such assurance. During much of the arms race, technological change
has served to help make second-strike forces more survivable,
and hence to stabilize the balance of terror. But the advent of
weapons like MIRVs with increasingly high accuracies threatens
to provoke new instability. Technological change, and the spread
of nuclear weapons to many countries that do not now have
them—the process called nuclear proliferation—could easily make
war more, not less, likely. Despite all precautions, accidental or
unauthorized firings of nuclear weapons by an insubordinate
military commander or by a terrorist group could trigger full-
scale nuclear destruction. Magnifying the number of weapons
also immensely complicates the problems of command and control involved in any effort to limit nuclear war once it has begun.
These problems will be more severe as poorer countries, unable
to spend billions of dollars on good command and control systems (like those of America and the USSR) possess such weapons. Nuclear war *can* happen.

Research on the question of whether arms races lead to war
has until recently been inconclusive. People have taken sides on
the issue with evidence that was no better than the maxims of
conventional wisdom (such as "If you would have peace, pre-
pare for war") and selective reference to contradictory examples.
Some people have argued there is no evidence that arms races
typically resulted in war. But a major survey of arms races and
deterrence efforts over long periods of history concluded that
the opposite was not true, either; that is, military deterrence did
not typically prevent the outbreak of war. Analysts of World
War I generally believe that the arms races before 1914 played
a significant role in bringing on the war.

More interestingly, a study of great powers' behavior since 1815 examined all the 99 "serious disputes" among them, serious disputes being carefully defined as military confrontations—mobilizations, blockades, seizures of territory, and the like—not severe enough to qualify as full-scale wars. Of these 99 disputes, however, 26 did result in the outbreak of full-scale war between great powers. A total of 28 of these disputes were preceded by an arms race (accelerating rates of growth in arms expenditures) by the confronting powers over the previous ten-year period; the other 71 were not. The striking finding of this analysis was that 82 percent of the disputes arising during accelerating arms races ended in war, whereas only 4 percent of the disputes not characterized by arms races ended in war.[14]

	Arms Race	No Arms Race
War	23	3
No War	5	68

This evidence is basically correlational; that is, it shows that arms races tend to be followed by war, but it does not pin down the cause. It still is possible to argue, for instance, that states engaged in the arms races were experiencing such conflict and tension, regardless of their military buildups, that they would have gone to war anyway. By this argument, the arms race was a symptom, not a cause, of the conflict that ended in war. While we cannot absolutely prove this argument is wrong, we now know without much question that engaging in an arms race is a very unreliable way to prevent a war.

To understand the relationship between arms races and war, we need to understand the process by which wars often come about. Essentially, periods of rapid change in military capabilities, and especially changes in one major power's capabilities relative to another major power, are likely to be very dangerous. The risks multiply when changes are also occurring in the wider international system, that is, when alliances are shifting, with old alliances weakening and new relationships among states being formed.

One study, which looked at the international system over the period of 1815 to 1970, found that periods of changing alliances tended to be followed very shortly by periods of more than the usual number of wars. Specifically, increases in the *tightness* of alliances were associated with more wars than usual, though decreases in alliance tightness tended to be followed by fewer wars. "Tightness" in this context means the degree to which all members of an alliance system are bound to one another by alliances or other links. A very tight system would be one in which all members of the Rio Pact in the Western Hemisphere were allied not only with one another and with the United States but also with the United States' allies in other parts of the world, such as NATO, Japan, South Korea, and Australia. Fully 84 percent of wars in the twentieth century were preceded by periods when the system grew tighter.[15]

The reason for this may be rooted in how decision makers process information. Decision makers must make estimates about the relative gains or losses they can expect if they take various actions. A rational decision maker will choose the action promising the greatest gain or the least loss. That estimate of probable gain or loss is made up of two elements: the absolute gain or loss if an act succeeds, and the probability of success. In at least some rough way, both of these elements, absolute value and probability, are included in the calculations we (as well as political decision makers) must make. The gain from a war fought to win rule over the world might be high if the war were successful, but most decision makers would consider the probability of success low and the losses in case of failure severe. Most decision makers, therefore, would not start such a war. Similarly, if for $1000 you could buy a chance to win $1 million, the attractiveness of the bet would depend on whether you thought the odds of success were ten to one or a million to one.

In making such estimates, a political decision maker has to think about the relative power of his or her own state, enemies, and allies. The probability that allies will help, and the probability that the enemy's allies will help the enemy, must be considered. Tightening blocs imply that alliance patterns are clearer, and so allies' behavior is more predictable. Increased tightness

may come by upgrading already existing ties or by adding new, highly committed allies. The leader of one alliance may see his or her strength significantly increased and expectations of winning a war improved, especially if the tightness occurs in an imbalanced fashion (more for one alliance than for the other). The leader thus becomes more willing to embark on war.[16]

This perspective on the importance of changes in systems as leading to war is supported by a careful look at the case of Europe before World War I. The period 1900–1914 saw steps toward increasing polarization, notably the addition of previously unallied England to the entente of France and Russia, increases in the tightness of the opposing alliances, and a shift in relative capabilities in favor of the entente.[17]

J. David Singer, reviewing all international crises and wars since 1815, reports that, although only 13 percent of all major-power militarized disputes in that period escalated into war, 75 percent of disputes ended in war when the parties were approximately equal in military power *and* there was a rapid military buildup in the three years preceding the dispute—in other words, when states of near-equal power were engaged in an arms race.[18]

States that are farthest apart on measures of power are least likely to become engaged in armed conflict. Both sides can easily calculate who would win in a military showdown, and the weaker is likely to give in to all but the most extreme demands. Of course, the weaker side does not always give in, as we saw in confrontations between the United States and North Vietnam and between the United States and Iran. Nor does the stronger state always win a war. Such factors as geographical distance, national morale, and a state's organizational efficiency make a difference and complicate simple calculations. Nevertheless, international violence is more likely among states that are roughly equal on measures of power, such as GNP, military manpower, defense expenditure, and energy production.

In a classic statement about this phenomenon, A.F.K. Organski argued that "nations are reluctant to fight unless they believe they have a good chance of winning, but this is true for both sides only when the two are fairly evenly matched, or at least

they believe they are."[19] Organski focuses on the period of "power transition," when a rising "challenger" comes to approximate, or nearly so, the power of a previously dominant state. "If great change occurs within a single lifetime, both challenger and dominant nation may find it difficult to estimate their relative power correctly, and may stumble into a war that would never have been fought if both sides had foreseen where the victory would lie."[20] It is the condition of change that affects calculations of relative power. The challenger may start a war because it thinks that now, for the first time, it has a good chance to win. Or, the dominant power may overestimate its strength (on the basis of its past power) or foresee its strength declining in the future; so it calculates that it is better off fighting now, even though it has lost some relative power, than in the future, when its position may be significantly worse. By this interpretation, it is the fact of *change during a period of near equality* that makes war likely, not just the fact of power equality itself. Change makes calculations of power and war outcome difficult because the evidence is ambiguous (even though the decision makers may not see the ambiguity). Decision makers especially may miscalculate when the rate at which an increase or decrease in relative power slows or speeds up. Miscalculation then may lead small wars to escalate into big ones, so this is a time when *major* wars are especially likely.

Organski also suggests that "a rapid rise in power . . . produces dissatisfaction in itself."[21] This means that the newly powerful state has not yet acquired the respect or status its leaders feel are due it as one of the most powerful countries; its military and economic strength are not yet matched by deference and recognition. (Recall the 15- or 20-year-long periods before the Communist regimes of the Soviet Union and China were granted full diplomatic recognition by other major powers.) Again, it is changing conditions, not merely static balances, that tend to create the risk.

What do we make of this under the current conditions? The relative power of the two big alliance systems has changed significantly, from a situation where the American bloc was much greater than that of the Soviet Union to one where they are

more nearly equal. Changes in the relative strength of the two alliance systems have stemmed from differing internal rates of economic growth as well as from the addition or loss of allies. Japan and most of Western Europe have grown very rapidly, the Soviet Union less so, and the United States still less. There have also been important changes in the composition and tightness of the alliances. American allies in Europe and Japan, while recovering their economic strength, have also regained their political independence from the United States. The alliance between China and the Soviet Union has been broken and replaced with a tacit alignment between China and the United States. The shift in oil prices (more than a tenfold increase in the last decade) has given formerly dependent American allies, such as Iran and Saudi Arabia, great economic power and the potential for substantial military independence.

Looking at this from an alliance viewpoint and the findings referred to above, recent changes toward a looser system of alliances would seem much more encouraging than would changes toward a tighter system—as long as the trend continues in the loosening direction, the chances of war would not increase and would perhaps even diminish somewhat. That America might be left without her important allies would surely seem very threatening, especially if the Soviet Union should establish tight discipline over its allies in Eastern Europe and elsewhere. But a general tightening of alliances (including, for example, a firm, explicit alliance between America and China, which would leave the Soviet Union with a feeling of irreversible encirclement) might be equally dangerous.

Looking at the immediate power balance of the two superpowers alone gives more reason for concern. Rapid changes in their relative power positions have occurred. The Soviet Union, long behind, has caught up to a position not worse than essential equivalence, with a complex arsenal of weaponry prohibiting any easy assessment of where the balance lies. In numbers of launching vehicles, in numbers and megatonnage of ICBMs, and in numbers of soldiers and armored vehicles, the Soviet forces are clearly ahead. In numbers of warheads and accuracy of missiles, in numbers and delivery capability of bombers, and

in sophistication of submarine missile-launching systems, the Americans are ahead. Each side is making vast efforts to build its advantages and strengthen its weaknesses. The American government has decided that it cannot risk allowing the Soviet Union to move its position of essential equivalence into a position of strategic predominance.

Also worrisome are the current alarms about the vulnerability of land-based missiles. We have seen strong arguments about why that vulnerability is exaggerated. Nevertheless, fears about vulnerability raise the risk that in a crisis, one superpower or the other may be tempted to strike, not because it wants a war, but because it fears the other may be about to attack. Both powers are taking vigorous actions to reduce their vulnerability, but some of the actions (like installing highly accurate MX missiles in fixed silos) may actually magnify the overall instability. Furthermore, major new arms programs may lead either power (or both) to fear that the long-term strategic balance will shift irrevocably against it. Someone, someday, may be tempted to strike before such a threatened shift can take effect. All these uncertainties are compounded by the complexities of modern weapons, the incomparability of the two arsenals, and the secrecy covering both sides' (but especially the Soviets') capabilities and intentions.

Knowing the fears that inevitably must arise during an arms race—fears that the other side will obtain some decisive advantage—it is hard not to believe that, on balance, the arms race leads to still greater tensions that may, particularly in periods of crisis, result in the outbreak of war. The events of August 1914 combined the preexisting anxieties and tensions of an arms race with those of the political crisis following the archduke's assassination. Indeed, the problem of instability in crisis, when tensions may erupt into a rapid spiral of fear, threat, and the initiation of violence, rests at the heart of many analysts' concerns about the stability of contemporary deterrence. In their view, the assumptions of rational behavior on which deterrence theory rests apply best to periods of relative calm in relations between nations. If so, deterrence works best when it is least needed!

Turrets coming off the production line for the American M1 Abrams main battle tank. (Courtesy of General Dynamics.)

Turrets coming off the production line for the American M1 Abrams main battle tank. (Courtesy of General Dynamics.)

4

Why Do Arms Races Occur?

Diplomacy without armaments is like music without instruments.

Frederick the Great, King of Prussia

Why do countries arm themselves, and how might an arms race possibly be controlled? The idea of a spiraling arms race represents an advance over the ideas prevalent in the early cold war years, when it seemed to many Americans that the phenomenon of action and reaction was all one way—that is, that America was reacting to Soviet aggressive actions and militarism. But when the period of isolation under Stalin drew to a close and Soviet and American scientists began to make contact with each other, it became apparent that Soviet citizens typically held a mirror image of that view; that is, they saw the Soviet Union simply as reacting to American threats. From this exchange, people developed a more general understanding that, in some real sense, each side was reacting to the other. It is very hard to sort out particular causes, especially once the action–reaction process is well under way.

After the first shocks of the cold war in the early post–World War II years, the Soviet and American military spending levels

were more or less constant for a long time, not showing a clear upward move again until the 1960s. An arms race, of course, need not imply an upward spiral, but it does imply competition. If two long-distance runners maintain a steady pace, we consider them to be in a race just as much as if their speed were continually increasing; it is the element of competition, or interaction, that makes the race.

In some degree, at least, that interaction is present in Soviet and American behavior—not a steady interaction, perhaps, but more likely one that moves in fits and starts in response to particular acts that seem especially provocative. The notion of a race surely does not explain every element of this behavior. It may tell us about the fact of interaction in arms spending but not about the level at which the interaction takes place; that is, the Soviet–American arms race might conceivably occur at spending levels of less than $50 billion a year instead of more than $200 billion. Something other than mere interaction must be affecting that level. Moreover, the idea of interaction does not explain what happened in the 1970s. The idea of interaction would lead us to expect the Soviet Union to moderate its military spending once the Americans slowed down after Vietnam. No such moderation occurred; rather, quite the contrary. Again, something else was going on. A variety of domestic and international pressures played a role.

International hostility may help get an arms race started and maintain it once it has begun, but various kinds of domestic influences also help maintain high levels of military spending. To understand further what drives this infernal machine, we must consider several kinds of explanations.

INTERNATIONAL INFLUENCES

Figure 4-1 is a schematic representation of the causes of military expenditures. It has been adapted from a diagram that Nazli Choucri and Robert C. North devised to provide a comprehensive framework for the causes of World War I.[1] Choucri and North were not so much concerned with explanations why par-

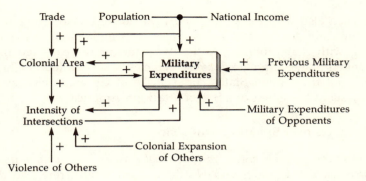

Figure 4-1
A model of the causes of military expenditures. [Adapted from Nazli Choucri and Robert C. North, *Nations in Conflict: National Growth and International Violence* (San Francisco: W. H. Freeman and Company. Copyright © 1975), p. 168.]

ticular decision makers behaved as they did in the course of the August 1914 crisis. Rather, they were trying to identify the larger conditions within governments, societies, and the whole international system that brought about the crisis.

This is a complex diagram, as international politics really is very complex. Each of the arrows with a plus sign (+) indicates a causal relationship, where an increase in a factor or variable helps produce an increase in the factor or variable to which the arrow points. In some cases, changes in a variable are caused by changes in two or more other variables. For example, the box labeled *Military Expenditures* has five arrows pointing to it. One arrow leads from *Military Expenditures of Opponents*. Considering the Soviet–American antagonism, we have a reference to one of the kinds of arms race phenomena that we have been discussing.

Obviously, the largest, most important, and potentially most threatening opponents are most relevant to military spending decisions. The plural *opponents* reminds us that we should not see all arms races purely as bilateral or two-country phenomena. In the contemporary world, the Soviet Union has to be con-

cerned also with the power and behavior of its close neighbor China and devotes a significant part of its military effort to coping with that problem. And it was not many years ago that United States strategic delivery vehicles were pointed at China so that the United States could strike at China as well as at Russia in the event of a Soviet attack on America.

Conflicts over Spheres of Influence

Two other arrows come from *Colonial Area* and *Intensity of Intersections*. For Choucri and North, the latter term refers to the "intensity of violence in specifically colonial conflicts between the actor state and other major powers."[2] In the late twentieth century, there are few colonial territories as such; most areas of the world are composed of formally sovereign states. Yet most major powers clearly do have "spheres of influence" consisting of states over which, to one degree or another, they exert substantial control. The Western Hemisphere (except for Cuba and maybe Nicaragua, which are very sore points) is such a sphere for the United States. Eastern Europe, with many Communist states that are often referred to as satellites of the Soviet Union, is of course the major USSR sphere of influence. But the two powers compete sharply with each other in these and other areas of the world. They are deeply involved in this competition, using economic, political, and military means in Africa, the Middle East, and Asia. In these contemporary intersections states frequently move from one power's sphere of influence to the other's in a process that often involves a great deal of military violence. Or, one power may repulse an effort to shift a state out of its sphere of influence, again often using substantial military force.

The Vietnam War is perhaps the most vivid example, but there are many others. Within the past few years, Ethiopia shifted from an American to a Soviet client, and its enemy and neighbor, Somalia, made the opposite shift in the course of a long and devastating war between them. After a long national liberation struggle, Angola ceased to be a colony of America's NATO ally, Portugal. Its struggle was heavily assisted by the Russians

and the Chinese, who each supported different, bitterly opposed local leaders. The United States and France later intervened to preserve their influence on Angola's African neighbor, Zaire, when there seemed to be some threat to it from Angola. Zimbabwe (Rhodesia) was long wracked by civil war. The government was dominated in various degrees by the white minority, who looked—not always successfully—to the West for help, and by the black guerrillas, who were helped, though not dominated, by the USSR. Western-backed Yemen fought Soviet-supported South Yemen on the Arabian peninsula. Of course, the United States and the Soviet Union have been deeply enmeshed in the Arab–Israeli conflict, sending arms to various and sometimes shifting allies. The Soviet Union helped engineer a coup against a fairly neutralist regime in Afghanistan to bring that country securely into its sphere of influence. The new regime proved highly unpopular, and the Russians found themselves increasingly drawn into that civil war. In Indochina, the Soviet Union helped the Vietnamese overthrow a government in Cambodia that had been allied with China.

Colonial or sphere-of-influence expansion and intense intersections feed into a demand for more military expenditures: If a big power has colonies or spheres of influence, it will need troops to police them. They may be troops of the big power itself or local client forces armed and supplied by the big power. If wars are going on or are threatened in various parts of the globe, the big states need arms and troops. If they don't fight directly, they still need arms to supply their small-power clients and money to support their clients' armed forces in war.

In each of these two relationships (military expenditures and colonial area; military expenditures and intersections) there are two arrows running between the pairs, one arrow in either direction. This indicates that two variables interact with each other in a positive way, creating feedback whereby not only does high intensity of intersection create a need or demand for more arms but the military expenditures also create the possibility of further intense intersections. With a large, well-trained, well-equipped, and mobile military establishment, there comes a potential—and perhaps a temptation—to use it. Many critics of

American foreign and security policy have maintained that the Vietnam War was made possible by, and in some sense perhaps caused by, the fact that the United States had developed a great capacity for fighting counterinsurgent or antiguerrilla wars in faraway places. These critics therefore tried to reduce the size of the American military establishment, and especially its capacity for fighting conventional wars, as a means of making it less likely that the United States would get involved in such wars. Whatever the merits of their evaluation of the Vietnam situation, it does seem reasonable that there would be a positive interaction between these two variables—local conflicts being made possible by, as well as stimulating, military expenditures.

Intersections may also escalate into serious military conflicts between major powers. This has rarely happened in the post–World War II international system. The United States and the Soviet Union so far have avoided head-on military violence, but the Soviet Union and China did fight a limited direct conflict on their common border, the Ussuri River, in 1969. Such violent superpower confrontations, if they do not lead immediately to all-out war, provide a further impetus to arms acquisitions for both contending powers.

Action–Reaction Processes

The idea of an arms race captures the sense that opposing states may be driven, from fear of permitting the other to gain an advantage, into an even sharper and perhaps ultimately self-defeating competition. This perspective on competition emerges also in the action–reaction perspective on arms races associated with the work of Lewis Frye Richardson.[3] Richardson was an English mathematician, physicist, and meterologist (as well as a member of the Society of Friends) who in the 1930s turned his skills to understanding the causes of international conflict. His work provided innovations in both theory building and statistical hypothesis testing, but he is probably most famous for the set of equations for arms races that now are typically referred to as "Richardson processes." In their simplest form, the equations read:

$$\Delta X = kY - aX + g \qquad (1)$$
$$\Delta Y = lX - bY + h \qquad (2)$$

In this two-nation arms race, the changes (Δ) in the military allocations of the nations (X and Y) are influenced by three major factors: (1) the military expenditures of the other state (k and l represent reaction coefficients); (2) the economic burden of paying for previous decisions to purchase military goods (a and b represent "fatigue" coefficients to indicate the weight of this burden); and (3) the underlying "grievance" held by each state against the other (g and h).

By this formulation, changes in state X's spending result, in the first term, from the degree of threat produced by the level of military expenditures of Y. This raises the level of X's expenditures, which thereby leads to an increase in Y's military spending. So too do the grievances—basic sources of political, economic, and ideological hostility. The result from these two terms alone would be a never-ending spiral, which of course does not happen in reality. Rather, the arms race may end in violent conflict—war—or it may for some reason be brought under control and stabilized or may even be reversed.

The last term in each of the equations is meant to indicate influences that affect the possibility of nonviolent damping of the race. The fatigue coefficients for the burden of expenditures represent the fact that arms spending diverts resources from civilian needs (consumption and investment) and cannot proceed to the point where it consumes the entire economy. Instead, the economic drain will stimulate political responses that, in the absence of war, can slow and ultimately stop the military expansion. The operation of such possible constraints can be seen faintly in the political efforts during 1982 to hold down military spending, efforts which were begun soon after congressional approval of administration tax cuts and budgetary requests, as the economic burden of the military budget increases became more apparent. Similarly, there is repeated speculation about the ability of the Soviet government to extract further resources for the military out of its civilian economy, especially

in the face of stagnating growth and the possibility of civilian unrest, as demonstrated in its neighbor Poland.

These fatigue constraints, however, may not be very powerful, especially at the relatively low levels of military spending experienced in the superpowers at present. Currently, the United States is spending about 7 percent of its GNP for military purposes; it spent about 13 percent during the height of the Korean War and over 40 percent at the peak of World War II. States under the direst threat may persuade their citizens to spend even more. Britain and the Soviet Union spent as much as 60 percent of their total product on defense during the worst of World War II; by that standard the current figure of about 14 percent for the USSR may not seem high. Israel has maintained a defense burden above 25 percent of its GNP for quite a few years (though with a good deal of foreign assistance contributing to its defense budget). Thus it is not clear how effective these constraints may currently be, particularly if the national sense of threat, or grievance, is high or can be made high.

This last reminds us of the importance of domestic *and* international politics in affecting arms races. Domestic elites may try to rally their people to meet a foreign threat. The Soviet government, with its relatively comprehensive control over the mass media of its people, can effectively propagandize about threats to socialism or Soviet national interests. American elites may, even without such tight control of the media, try the same, as in Senator Arthur Vandenberg's advising President Truman, at the beginning of the cold war, to "go and scare hell out of the country." Once these popular passions are unleashed, policymakers may even become more constrained by it than they wish to be: Recall the witch hunting and fears of the Joseph McCarthy era. Some Americans are afraid that the current revival of cold war sentiments may escalate into a new wave of virulent domestic anticommunism. The greater the sense of economic burden (fatigue), the greater the temptation to elites to justify that burden by fanning popular fears and grievances. Fatigue, therefore, cannot be depended upon to slow modern arms races.

DOMESTIC INFLUENCES

Shift now in Figure 4-1 to the influence, at the upper right corner, labeled *Previous Military Expenditures.* Pressures to maintain and to increase military expenditures arise within a country in at least three different ways.

Bureaucratic Politics

The leader of any large organization must be deeply concerned with the interests of his or her organization. A leader will be most reluctant to see the size of the organization shrink or its budget cut. Furthermore, the leader is likely to feel that the organization is doing important jobs for society—if he didn't think so, he probably would do something else for a living. If it is doing an important job and fulfilling an important function, then it would do even better with more people and resources at its disposal.

Moreover, the leader's own power in the government and in society at large depends heavily on the size of the organization. Leaders of big and growing organizations receive more respect than do leaders of small or shrinking ones. A leader will, therefore, vigorously resist any effort to cut the budget or personnel level of the organization and do his best to expand them. Research on budget making has long established that just about the best predictor of the size of an organization's budget in any year is the size of its last budget (with, especially in an expanding economy, an incremental increase).

Military organizations are by no means unique in this characteristic, but neither are they immune from it. Personal self-interest, interests of the organization one leads, and images of societal self-interest all influence the leader to ask for a higher budget. After all, if the Air Force Chief of Staff doesn't speak up to be sure that the Air Force gets a fair share of society's resources, who will? This also means that when one major weapons system becomes outmoded or obsolete, there will be a built-in interest group pressing either to modernize it and somehow keep it going or to replace it with something else that

will do a similar job and keep the same people and resources employed.

When the B-52 bomber becomes obsolete, Air Force generals will look around for a new bomber, such as the B-1, to replace it. They think the bombing mission is important and vital to American security: How can there be a good Air Force if there are no big, glamorous planes to fly? Who would enlist in the Air Force only to be a missile command officer in a silo hundreds of feet underground? Air Force evaluations of the merits of a proposed new strategic bomber are unlikely, therefore, to be entirely objective and disinterested.

The Air Force's major mission has evolved to one of strategic nuclear deterrence, which depends on land-based missiles. Air Force generals will be loath to see that element of the strategic triad abandoned as obsolete. They will look hard for something like the MX and a means to deploy it. Once a weapon has gone far through the process of research and development, it becomes politically and bureaucratically very difficult not to produce and deploy it in large numbers. For example, the MIRV was developed largely to ensure that some American retaliatory vehicles would be able to penetrate Soviet defenses even if the USSR should deploy an effective ABM system. The 1972 ABM Treaty between the United States and the USSR, however, very sharply limited ABM construction and made MIRVs unnecessary for the main purpose for which they were designed. Nevertheless, production and deployment of MIRV went ahead.

The Navy, too, has its own interests. Admirals like to maintain big surface ships like aircraft carriers as well as the limited-mission and not-so-glamorous nuclear submarines. It's hard to "join the Navy and see the world" from under the sea.

This is not to imply that such leaders are corrupt or that their advice to maintain or acquire a weapons system is necessarily mistaken: Their evaluation of the national interest and that of most objective observers might well coincide. But it does imply that the allocation of resources within a government—or the total allocation of society's resources to all government activities—is strongly resistant to change, especially in any downward direction. This year's military budget is a good predictor

(along with such external factors as intersections and opponents' spending) of next year's military budget.

Technological Momentum

Bureaucratic inertia is buttressed by technological momentum. Military research and development employs a half million of the best-qualified scientists and engineers worldwide and absorbs one-third to one-half of the world's human and material resources devoted generally to research and development. The research is intellectually challenging—and highly competitive. Individuals compete with one another, corporations and military services compete with their counterparts, and, of course, their countries compete. The incentives, privileges, and rewards are high. The work, however, takes a long time. Lead times of 10 years or more are typical from conceptualization through design, model production, improvement, repeated testing, evaluation, prototype production, training, and final deployment. This scientific inertia intertwines with bureaucratic inertia to make it very difficult to halt a promising project once it gets under way, even if its initial purpose (as with MIRV) has been lost.

The MIRV system had its origins in satellite-launching systems of the early 1960s. It began principally in government organizations: the Advanced Research Projects Agency of DOD, the Space Technology Laboratory, and the Air Force Space and Missile System Office. Once many of the pieces were available, it then became almost inevitable that they would be put together as a multiple-warhead delivery system, and private aerospace companies combined with the government laboratories and military chiefs to promote the project. As Herbert York, who observed the process from inside, remarked, "Once the technology was developed MIRV assumed a momentum of its own; the chances of halting it were by then slim."[3]

MIRV perhaps had its origin in technological momentum and was preserved, first, by action–reaction forces and, finally, by bureaucratic inertia. Sometimes a project may be stopped even though it is far down the technological ways, but that happens only rarely. Even ABM deployment, which was halted by the

1972 treaty, is not a clear case. In the forms under development up to that time, it clearly was a loser—technically incapable of effectively doing the job for which it was being developed. Recently, however, a new generation of technological possibilities, such as laser beams, are being touted for ABM application, and pressures to perfect and deploy them are apparent.

The Military–Industrial Complex

The third kind of domestic pressure, one that arises from the society and economy at large, is what is often referred to as the "military–industrial complex." In his last public address as President, Dwight Eisenhower warned about the political influence of a newly powerful military–industrial complex:

> We have been compelled to create a permanent armaments industry of vast proportions. Added to this, three-and-a-half million men and women were directly engaged in the defense establishment. We annually spend on military security alone more than the net income of all United States corporations.
>
> Now this conjunction of an immense military establishment and a large arms industry is new in the American experience. The total influence—economic, political, even spiritual—is felt in every city, every state house, every office of the federal government . . . . In the councils of government, we must guard against the acquisition of unwarranted influence, whether sought or unsought, by the military/industrial complex. The potential for the disastrous rise of misplaced power exists and will persist.

The phrase *military–industrial complex*, especially if interpreted broadly to include the labor unions and political leaders (such as members of Congress with defense industries or military bases in their districts, who would benefit directly from military spending) is now a commonly used expression. It represents the understanding that whether or not the American economic system benefits from assertive foreign or military policies, particular interest groups certainly do benefit. Even if the American economy as a whole could prosper without military spending, some industries and some geographical areas would suffer se-

Table 4-1
Personnel Transfers Between Department of Defense (DOD) and
Major Military Contractors, 1970–1979

Company	Total Flow	Flow to Company DOD Military	DOD Civilian	Flow To DOD
Boeing	398	316	35	37
General Dynamics	239	189	17	32
Grumman	96	67	5	16
Lockheed	321	240	30	34
McDonnell-Douglas	211	159	12	29
Northrop	360	284	50	16
Rockwell	234	150	26	47
United Technologies	83	50	11	12
Total	1942	1455	186	233

Source: Adapted from Gordon Adams, *The Iron Triangle: The Politics of Defense Contracting*
(New York: Council on Economic Priorities, 1981), p. 84.

vere short- or medium-term damage from any reduction of military expenditures.

Controversy surrounds the question of whether profits in the defense industries are higher than in comparable nondefense industries; overall there seems to be no conclusive evidence that they are.[5] Nevertheless, a cutback, disrupting production and marketing in these industries and forcing their firms to make and find buyers for alternative products, would cause sharp, temporary losses. Defense-industry corporations, aided by the technical and political knowledge of former military officers who become defense-industry employees (see Table 4-1), try hard to maintain their business and to add new contracts. They are helped by government policies that seek to maintain a mobilization base in defense industries, especially the aerospace industry. It is important, for instance, to have several firms capable of manufacturing modern military aircraft. When one of Lockheed's aviation contracts is finished, a new contract will be

needed if the company's experience, skilled labor, and capital equipment are not to be scattered and lost.

Increasingly, sales of arms abroad, especially to allies and the Third World, rival in economic importance the sales of many countries' arms manufacturers to their domestic governments. Especially during the post–Vietnam War years, arms exports became a major prop to the military–industrial complex. United States arms exports of $10 billion in 1974 and 1975 amounted to over half as much as the total of U.S. government arms purchases for the American armed forces. Foreign sales can make the difference between short production lines (building perhaps a few hundred tanks per year at high cost) or longer production lines (turning out a thousand or more tanks with the lower unit costs of mass production). These efficiencies of scale are especially important to smaller countries like France, who could not buy enough for their own armed forces to keep costs at a competitive level. Arms sales also are useful to help the balance of payments. American and European arms sales to Iran and the Arab states made a significant contribution to paying the increased cost of oil imports from those same countries. Both to sustain a healthy domestic arms industry and to help the balance of payments, governments of exporting countries often want to encourage arms exports at the same time that, for other reasons (such as the unsavory nature of some of the recipients' authoritarian regimes), they may wish to discourage them. Figure 4-2 shows the major arms exporting countries and the destinations of their weapons.

On the demand side, the governments of exporting countries usually want to use arms sales or military assistance programs to build up their foreign allies. South Korea and Saudi Arabia are very important allies of the United States, and the demands of American national security seem to override doubts about arming governments that will use those arms at least partly to oppress their own populations. Any government policy that tries to limit international arms sales always bumps up against these political and economic realities. And in most cases, if one country (the United States, for instance) refuses to sell arms to

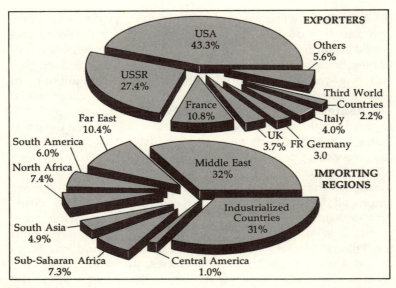

Figure 4-2
Shares of world exports (by country) and world imports (by region) of
major weapons, 1977–1980. [Stockholm International Peace Research
Institute (SIPRI), *World Armaments and Disarmament,* SIPRI Yearbook
1981 (London: Taylor and Francis, 1981), p. xxi.]

a Third World state, some other country (for example, France
or the Soviet Union) will gladly oblige.

Thus a variety of pressures help maintain a heavy flow of
military sales and assistance to Third World countries. Add the
desire of many governments for modern arms and police primarily as instruments to control their own population (rather
than to deter their neighbors) and the desire of industrialized
countries to help prop up the governments of their friends
(whether by the Russians in Afghanistan, Angola, or Ethiopia,
or the Americans in Morocco, the Philippines, or Zaire), and
the result is a powerful constellation of interests maintaining
the world's biggest industries.

Certainly someone stands to gain from every dollar spent on arms; some industries do benefit from military spending and would suffer from its reduction. The important question for military–industrial complex theories is how broad and deep that suffering would be compared with the benefits that might go to other industries if resources were taken away from military ends. The disarmament damage to military industries (and probably to certain regional labor markets as well) would exceed the gains going to any other single sector of industry; that is, while military spending does not necessarily benefit the economy as a whole, the gains from defense spending are greater to a few industries than are the costs to any one sector when spread among all the sectors of the civilian economy. Toy makers, citrus growers, and home builders all lose a little business when more money is spent for fighter planes. But if less money were spent for fighters, McDonnell-Douglas Corporation would lose heavily—and resist mightily. In democracies, pressure groups concentrate their activities on those issues that promise them the greatest gains and will not deeply resist efforts of other groups pursuing their most important special interests when those efforts involve modest costs (as long as the prospective costs *remain* modest). Each looks out for gaining something for himself and tolerates similar activities by others.

This essentially political explanation would account for continuing excessive levels of military spending (and perhaps even maintenance of an ideological climate of fear and hostility necessary to support such a defense posture), despite the fact that economic gains were limited to but a small segment of the economy. This view fits with the findings of a major study of American businessmen's attitudes toward tariff issues. According to the study's authors: "The men who feared loss from a tariff cut were more in favor of raising tariffs than were those who explicitly asserted that they would gain by the increase. We see that fear of loss is a more powerful stimulus than prospect of gain."[6]

Of course, similar interests are powerful in the Soviet Union. While there are no capitalists in that economy, certainly state industrial managers have interests in promoting the growth,

power, prosperity, and technological preeminence of the arms manufacturing plants they control. They too share interests with their clients in the Red Army and Strategic Rocket Forces and with hawkish ideologues in the Communist Party. A cold war—though not necessarily a hot one—helps to maintain their privileges and central roles in Soviet society. In both countries, therefore, entrenched economic and political interests serve to maintain the momentum of established hardline policies and to resist change. In a perverse way, the military–industrial complex of each country helps the other. Each embodies the foreign threat that its counterpart in the other country needs to justify its own activities.

A more radical argument holds that military spending undergirds modern industrial capitalist economies. By this line of reasoning, if it were not for the prop provided by military spending, industrial capitalism would quickly collapse into underconsumption. To absorb "surplus capital," the government must increase its spending and taxing. "Welfare state" spending is opposed by conservatives because it is thought to damage work incentives in the labor market and to compete unfairly with private enterprise. Expanded public spending for civil purposes therefore is not acceptable, but military spending is, precisely because it does not compete with big private vested interests.

It is difficult to make a satisfactory test of this idea. Nearly everyone agrees that rearmament for World War II provided a stimulus to the American economy that brought it out of the Depression. Since World War II, military spending as a proportion of GNP has been at a level previously unprecedented in peacetime, coinciding with a long period of prosperity. But other kinds of government spending, taxation, and monetary policy (as informed by modern economics) probably deserve more credit as causes of that prosperity. Some other countries, notably Japan and West Germany, have had even more expansive economies with much less military spending. Nevertheless, it is now well known that political leaders like to increase government spending just before elections to create at least short bursts of prosperity that will impress voters favorably. Military spending is

one that is relatively easy to increase and at most times is considered a proper function of government. Arthur Burns advised President Eisenhower of this in March 1960: "Burns' conclusion was that unless some decisive governmental action were taken, and taken soon, we were heading for another dip (in the economy), which would hit its low point just before the elections . . . . He urgently recommended that two steps be taken immediately: by loosening up credit and, where justifiable, increasing spending for national security."[7]

In an analysis of year-to-year military spending changes in the postwar United States, Miroslav Nincic and Thomas Cusack found that "military spending cut back at an expected rate of $2 billion per annum after on-year (presidential) elections and expanded at a similar rate in the two years prior to those elections."[8] Thus, although the underconsumption thesis seems not very plausible in general, political leaders will sometimes boost military spending for reasons that have more to do with politics and economics than with strictly military needs.

CONVERGENT PRESSURES

All these influences help explain why the lines for military spending shown in Figure 1-2 (in Chapter 1) generally maintained their levels or rose fairly steadily. Periods of significant reduction in military spending, while not totally absent, are rare. Usually a "ratchet effect" occurs from a war. After the level of military effort has been geared up to a high wartime level, a "ratchet" of bureaucratic and political–economic pressure keeps it from dropping down all the way to its prewar level. The new expenditure floor is usually well above that previous level. This happened in the United States after all its major wars in the last 90 years except the Vietnam War (that is, after the Spanish–American War, the two world wars, and the Korean War).

Finally, note in Figure 4-1 the fifth arrow leading to the *Military Expenditures* box. This one comes from *Population* interacting with *National Income*. We have not talked much about this particular influence, though we may take it as a suggestion of

various domestic influences. Here, it chiefly implies that economic and population growth provide the means for expanding the military establishment: A big country can support a big army. In a growing economy, more resources can be devoted to military purposes without necessarily reducing anyone's share of the expanding pie; maintaining large armed forces becomes relatively painless.

Population and income growth also remind us of some explanations—indicated at the upper left by the arrows leading to growth of *Colonial Area*—for imperialism. Growth not only provides the possibility of military expansion, it may also provide the need for it—a need for assured food supplies to feed a growing population or a need for assured raw materials to feed a growing economy. Every modern state depends for its popularity on being able to satisfy the rising demands of its citizens for material goods and services. Haunting all democratic governments is the spectre of the Great Depression of the 1930s. Economic failure destroyed democracy and brought Hitler to power in Germany, which raised the threat of dictatorship throughout Europe. The basic ideology of capitalism values economic growth and tolerates inequalities in the interest of providing incentives to ensure growth. The Communist states, as part of an increasingly interlinked world economy, could not escape this same pressure even if they wished. Through media of worldwide communication and the ever-more-porous "Iron Curtain," Soviet and Eastern European citizens are fully aware of the higher living standards of their western counterparts. Communist governments have to make some concessions to their citizens' demands; indeed, their claim to power depends, in large part, on their promise to provide their people with better living conditions than they had under the old capitalist order.

All industrialized countries, capitalist or communist, must have reliable access to supplies of food and raw materials if they are to ensure economic growth and the domestic political peace dependent on that growth. The United States is substantially, and increasingly, dependent on foreign sources of oil and such minerals as chromium, nickel, cobalt, manganese, and platinum. (see Figure 4-3). Western Europe is completely reliant on

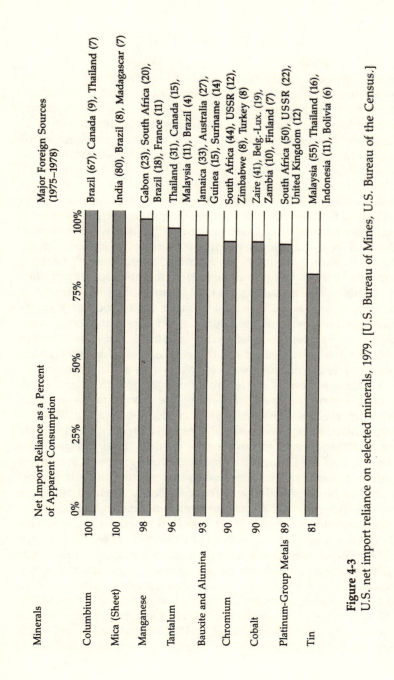

Figure 4-3
U.S. net import reliance on selected minerals, 1979. [U.S. Bureau of Mines, U.S. Bureau of the Census.]

imports for 10 vital raw materials; Japan, for 11. Many of these are secured from politically unstable areas in the Third World, especially in southern Africa and the Middle East. Decision makers must worry whether Third World governments will band together in cartels to raise the price of their raw material exports manyfold or engage in politically motivated boycotts of western consumers. The OPEC cartel for oil, with its higher prices and earlier boycott, is the prime example.

More threatening is the likelihood—or certainty—that many Third World governments will be unstable. If raw materials are to be exported, some government must be able to enforce social order. Mines must be kept open and supplied with electricity. Oil wells must be kept pumping. Railroads or pipelines must reliably carry the material to port, where ship-loading facilities must be maintained. Mass unrest or civil war can endanger the ability to keep these raw materials flowing, as in postrevolutionary Iran, where oil exports fell to hardly more than a tenth of their volume under the Shah. This kind of danger lies behind the demand for military forces able to intervene to prop up weak but "friendly" Third World regimes or possibly to ensure the continued operation of raw material supplies if the Third World government collapses. The American Rapid Deployment Force is designed for precisely this kind of use in the Middle East or elsewhere. It may seem all the more urgent knowing that another great power, such as the Soviet Union, may also intervene either to secure its own materials supplies or to deny vital supplies to the West. Alarmists speak of a "raw materials war," which calls up memories of pre–1914 spheres of influence, colonial expansion, and imperialism. Here, domestic influences— the need to maintain resource supplies for growth and political stability—combine with international pressures leading to similar needs of other states. Together, they produce international pressures of intense intersections such as those noted earlier in the chapter.

All told, domestic influences seem so strong that some analysts say that military establishments are essentially "autistic actors." They take this image from the psychology of autistic children, who shut themselves off almost completely from out-

side social stimuli and respond overwhelmingly to their own internal psyches. In this view, the arms race is not really a race at all, if by "race" we mean that the relative positions of the participants influence the pace at which they run. The government and industrial leaders in an "autistic" system would maintain a military buildup almost solely as a result of demands and pressures from within their own countries, not as a result of international incidents or military gains by the other racer. By this explanation, we are racing against ourselves; international events are irrelevant, except perhaps as they provide an excuse for societal elites to demand sacrifices for military purposes. What the enemy is doing thus would become useful domestic propanganda to support policies leaders desire on other grounds. Such an explanation would certainly not rule out even some collusion between the elites of the two ostensibly competing countries. For instance, at about the time one country's elites were considering budgetary appropriations or authorizations, the enemy might act aggressively or show off a new weapon to assist the elites in extracting more military funds; the enemy would then look for the same favor in return when its appropriation cycle came around.

Too exclusive a preoccupation with Soviet and American military spending may obscure another fact: Many countries have military establishments that say they are directed toward external enemies but really are chiefly directed toward internal enemies. They are not instruments of foreign war but instruments of internal repression. This is most obviously the case in many Third World countries, but even for the Soviet Union it should not be ignored. Political dissidence still calls forth repression. Half of the citizens of the Soviet Union are not Russians but are members of other European and Asian ethnic groups with a potential for nationalist separatism. The Soviet government would need a substantial army just to ensure internal security.

WHICH INFLUENCES ARE MOST IMPORTANT?

It is one thing to list these various influences that may promote military spending or militarism and quite another to decide how important each is. Most of the explanations seem plausible in one degree or another, and there is some evidence for each. Choucri and North report that, for the majority of major powers in the years before World War I, most of their arrows to *Military Expenditures* do turn out to identify significant relationships. But they see domestic factors as more powerful than international ones. In their words:

> The primary importance of domestic factors . . . does not preclude the reality of arms competition. Two countries whose military establishments are expanding largely for domestic reasons can, and indeed almost certainly will, become acutely aware of each other's spending. Thereafter, although spending may continue to be powerfully influenced by domestic factors, deliberate military competition may increase and even take the form of an arms race (although the race may be over specific military features and may be a very small portion of total military spending).[9]

Richardson applied his model to information on the Anglo–German rivalry immediately preceding World War I, but he had only a handful of data points that could be interpreted to fit a variety of possible equations. Others since then, like Choucri and North, have done better work on the pre–1914 rivalries and on more recent arms races. Most efforts, not surprisingly, have concentrated largely on the post–World War II Soviet–American (or occasionally, NATO–Warsaw Pact) arms race. The basic Richardson equations have been modified to produce political explanations that seem more plausible. For example, instead of saying that the change in military spending depends on the *level* of the rival's spending, one can make it depend on the *change* in the rival's level of spending or on the *ratio* of one's own spending to that of the rival. Or, one can recognize that spending in any one year goes in part to maintain existing forces and in part to add to them. More important than current levels of spending, therefore, may be the existing stock of weapons to which any

addition may be made. In periods when the United States maintained a stock of strategic weapons far superior to that of the
Soviet Union, American presidents could (perhaps mistakenly)
be relaxed about high levels of Soviet spending in any one year—
it might take many years of high spending levels to bring the
Soviet weapons stock to essential equivalence with that of the
United States.

Efforts to take account of the triangular nature of superpower
interactions have been especially intriguing. So too have efforts
to couple the action–reaction of military spending with the action–reaction of international political and military initiatives.
Richard Ashley adapted the Choucri–North model to the U.S.–
Soviet–China relationship. He concluded that the United States
partly responded to Soviet spending; he also found a large measure of inertia sustained by the domestic military establishment
and national security bureaucracy. The Soviet Union's military
spending patterns were a little different. They seemed to be
dominated by domestic forces and not to respond in any regular
way at all to American military spending. Neither country's military budgets seemed to respond much to what Choucri and
North called intersections of interest. Ashley, however, measured these as *commercial* intersections, and that may well be
too limited a definition, missing the *confrontations* that have occurred between the superpowers in Africa and elsewhere. He
did find some Soviet response to *Chinese* military spending after
the two great Communist states broke off relations, and he found
some Chinese reaction to collisions of interest with the USSR.[10]
Other analysts have also found that, in the Soviet–American
(or, sometimes, the Soviet–American–Chinese) case, the main
effects are exerted by domestic rather than international forces.[11]

These results, derived as they are from somewhat different
theories and research procedures, seem to converge on an
agreement that international influences on arms races are less
powerful than Richardson's early analyses would have us expect. Instead, they drive explanation most importantly to some
combination of bureaucratic inertia and the broader *domestic* forces
implied by one version or another of military–industrial complex
perspectives. Perhaps the superpowers may respond not to

"normal" increments in each other's military posture but only to major changes in their bilateral realtions.

The United States did react with increased military expenditures to international political reversals on certain occasions: It rearmed after the North Korean attack on South Korea in 1950; it started a crash program in the late 1950s when Soviet space achievements suggested—erroneously—that Russia might be about to get an ICBM first-strike capability; and American foreign policy reversals of the late 1970s, especially in the Middle East, helped stimulate the most recent American arms buildup. The Soviets, for their part, may have boosted their military spending in the 1960s in response to the visible and rather humiliating defeat they suffered in the Cuban missile crisis—"never again" to have to yield. Yet even in those cases, the new arms exertions had already been demanded by many domestic interests. The external political reversals provided a rallying cry, an excuse, as much as a true impetus.

Many problems arise in trying to do a good arms-race analysis. The results can rarely be conclusive. The time period for analysis is relatively short. The data available are highly aggregated; usually one must deal with total military spending rather than, say, spending for strategic arms, which might be the most relevant to an arms race analysis. The quality of the data on Soviet military spending is very poor, subject to wide differences in estimation. Data may be selected to bias the results, and different estimates provide the basis for quite different conclusions. In western countries, the time lags between request, authorization, and appropriation make it hard to identify a response to any particular external stimulus. Some military programs are undertaken in anticipation of, rather than reaction to, opponents' programs. As a result, any analysis is bound to contain a substantial element of error. Moreover, both the bureaucratic politics and arms race explanations lead us to expect very similar behavior, namely, steady or gradually increasing levels of expenditure for both sides. Given the problems with data quality, few time points, and so forth, it is very hard to pick apart different patterns and to document those differences in a convincing way.

In the present state of the art and science, probably the best we can say is that both domestic and action–reaction international influences do operate and do make a difference. Evidence seems to tip toward giving somewhat greater weight to internal influences. There is also evidence that the Soviet government's arms spending is constrained by inadequate output, particularly at certain phases of the cycle of five-year plans. Civilian needs seem to get greater emphasis at the beginning of each plan and at the end, as producers are trying to meet plan targets; military spending fares best in the middle years. American military spending may be affected by a different kind of internal political cycle—one keyed to election years. Neither of these cyclical patterns, however, is firmly established.

Finally, behavior varies according to who the decision makers are; that is, certain leaders or administrations may be more tolerant of military spending by the other side or less willing to divert funds from domestic civilian needs than are others. Evidence has been found for this during the naval race between the two world wars.[12] Most recently, we see it with the Reagan administration. The current administration has not only decided to initiate a vast increase in military spending, but it has tried to accomplish it by cutting domestic spending while avoiding raising taxes. This was a deliberate political choice; thus it *does* matter who is in charge.

Since the empirical results are not conclusive, and since each of the "independent" or "causal" influences is itself caused by prior factors in the chain, it becomes very hard to suggest effective ways to reduce arms expenditures and slow what we call the arms race. Some people, accepting one version of the autism argument, insist that only a drastic change in domestic economic, social, and political institutions could make a difference. But since both the United States and the Soviet Union behave similarly despite their very different domestic systems, that prescription becomes questionable. Obviously, some shift in popular and elite preferences and sense of threat would help—but how much?

During the Vietnam War, American popular opinion toward the military shifted enormously. In the earlier cold war years,

typically less than 20 percent of the population wanted to see defense expenditures reduced; according to national surveys in 1969 and 1970, that proportion was up to about half the population. Popular opposition to the military played a central role in reducing military expenditures after the Vietnam War; for the first time in over a hundred years, U.S. military spending after a war dropped below the floor typical of the years preceding the war. But by the late 1970s, in response to dramatic American foreign policy reversals in Africa, Iran, and Afghanistan and the absence of any Soviet restraint in military spending, American opinion shifted again. Popular attitudes on this issue shift often and respond strongly to mass media treatment of foreign events. The Iranian hostage affair, for instance, became a television spectacular that importantly fed Americans' determination to recover their military muscle. After it was over and the domestic costs of new arms programs became apparent, enthusiasm for military spending once again waned (see Figure 4-4).

Further attention to governmental and bureaucratic sources of arms momentum clearly is in order, as is attention to the forces of technological momentum. Would it be easier to restrain scientific research and development than to head off bureaucratic pressures to deploy newly developed systems? Clearly the international side of the explanation deserves attention. New ways to reduce conflict between competing states, to encourage communication, and to verify arms control agreements—so we can see what the Russians are doing and not simply have to trust them (or they us)—are essential. Some possible actions of this sort will be discussed in later chapters.

Negotiations for arms control have proved exceptionally difficult—gestation of the SALT II treaty occupied eight years and produced a stillborn runt. Sometimes there is a role for one-sided acts of self-control—limited acts, to be sure—and for acts that can be reversible if they fail to bring forth corresponding tit-for-tat concessions from the other side. The role of political actions—colonial expansion and intersections as a direct influence on military spending patterns—should not be neglected. The increase in American military spending in 1980 seemed to be more in response to Soviet acts in Afghanistan and elsewhere

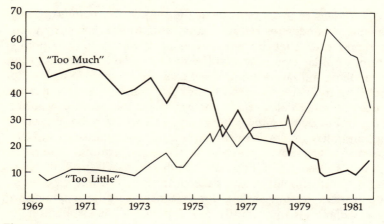

Figure 4-4
Public preferences for increased or reduced U.S. defense spending, 1969–1981. When two or more surveys were made in the same month, the plotted point represents the average. [Bruce Russett and Donald R. DeLuca, " 'Don't Tread on Me': American Opinion on Foreign Policy in the Eighties," *Political Science Quarterly*, 96, 3 (1981):384; and recent CBS/NYT and NBC/AP surveys.]

than simply to changes in Soviet spending. In any case, because the arms race is a complex phenomenon, with several causes, we cannot expect to find any single solution.

Adversaries and partners: Presidents Ronald Reagan and Leonid Brezhnev. (Richard Kalvar/©Magnum Photos, Inc.; ©Semyon Raskin/Magnum Photos, Inc.)

5

Conflict and Cooperation in the Arms Race

He was, so to speak, both my partner and my adversary.

Nikita Khrushchev,
speaking about John F. Kennedy,
in *Khrushchev Remembers:*
The Last Testament

THE PRISONERS' DILEMMA

We now must do some rather complex analytical work to understand how nuclear politics can create dilemmas from which there may be no satisfactory exit. Our analysis will use a perspective on arms races that comes from the theory of games and is especially popular in the form called "the prisoners' dilemma." It shows how people (including the leaders of nations) can become trapped in self-defeating acts. It stresses interdependent choice in the combination of conflict and cooperation found in many social situations. Game theory, if used carefully, can allow us to think essentially in terms of equivalence of roles: "How would my behavior look if I were in the other person's shoes?" It may help us avoid the perspective that simply says: "We can only be provoked; he must be deterred."

We begin by thinking about conflict and cooperation situations as mixed-motive, or non-zero-sum, games—meaning sit-

uations where the combined value of the outcomes to each of two players is other than zero. These are situations in which it is possible to have many outcomes where both players lose or gain. By contrast, in zero-sum games one person's gain equals the other's loss; when they are added together, the sum is always zero. (We are assuming that gains and losses can be measured in some common unit. In many situations, this is a serious simplification; in others, where one may speak of gains and losses in terms of money or years in prison, the simplification is less damaging.)

In most of the games we play for sport, such as chess or tennis, winning or losing is not everything. Even when we lose the match, presumably we gain from the exercise and the pleasure of the competition. In international relations, too, it is a mistake to think of most conflicts as zero-sum situations. On the contrary, two countries often gain something from staying at peace, and both would usually incur serious losses from going to war. Peaceful coexistence is precisely such a situation. Both big powers continue to compete and to gain or lose power at the expense of the other, but they also have an interest in keeping the competition from becoming militarily or economically destructive to both of them. We shall explore some conditions that may encourage or hinder cooperative behavior, starting with an imaginary example of criminal behavior and then applying it to situations of international politics.

In the basic story of the prisoners' dilemma, two people are arrested. Each is held incommunicado in a police station after an armed robbery and murder have been committed. Each person is presented with a pair of unattractive options, and each is questioned separately and given a choice by the police official: "I'm pretty sure that you two were responsible for the killing, but I don't have quite enough evidence to prove it. If you will confess first and testify against the other prisoner, I will see that you are set free without any penalty, and he will be sentenced to life imprisonment. On the other hand, I am making the same proposal to him, so if he confesses first, you will be the one to spend life in prison and he will go free. If you both confess on the same day, we will have a little mercy. But you still will be

badly off, because you will both be sentenced to 20 years in prison for armed robbery. If you both want to be stubborn, we cannot convict you for a major crime, but we can punish you for a small crime you committed in the past—one that carries a one-year prison term. If you want to take a chance that your fellow prisoner will keep quiet, go ahead. But if he doesn't— and you know what sort of criminal he is—you will do very badly. Think it over."

In order to analyze these problems, we shall illustrate the dilemma with a simple table.

Prisoners' Dilemma

		Leon	
		Cooperate	Defect
Ron	Cooperate	*2, 2 (R, R)*	*4, 1 (S, T)*
	Defect	*1, 4 (T, S)*	*3, 3 (P, P)*

Each box represents the outcome that will occur if two players, Ron and Leon, choose the strategies that lead to it. The first number represents the outcome for Ron; the second, for Leon. A *1* is the best possible outcome; a *4*, the worst. The letters represent the payoffs (again, the first for Ron and the second for Leon). *R* is reward received; *P* is punishment received; *T* is the temptation to defect when the opponent cooperates; and *S* labels the opponent as a sucker (or a saint, as you prefer).

What will the prisoners do in the situation described? Since they cannot communicate with each other, each must make the best possible choice regardless of what the other does. In terms of rational self-interest according to the theory of games, each should act so that he will get the better of the two possible outcomes for each of his opponent's choices. Consider Ron's options, for example: If Leon should confess (that is, defect from his partnership with Ron), Ron will get a 20-year term (a 3) if he too defects, but life imprisonment (a 4) if he keeps quiet (that is, tries to cooperate with Leon). Hence Ron is better off if he defects. If, on the contrary, Leon should cooperate, Ron receives a 1-year sentence (a 2) if he too cooperates, but gets off free (a

1) if he defects. Again, Ron is better off defecting. In fact, *whatever* Leon does, Ron does better by defecting; so, by this logic, he will confess. Leon—in the same situation—will also confess. As a consequence of their cold-blooded rationality, both will receive 20-year sentences! Jointly, they will end up much worse off than they might have had they been able to coordinate their strategies and had each been able to depend on the other to cooperate. This is the prisoners' dilemma.

This basic style of analysis can be applied to many kinds of international politics problems, especially in settings of arms races and crisis behavior.[1] To do so, however, we will have to move from a situation where we have easily measured outcomes (years of prison sentence) to one where it is harder to attach precise numbers to outcomes. In war we may speak about billions of dollars of damage done or thousands of people killed, but it is hard to combine dollars and people into a single sum. And, of course, there are other values (such as justice, freedom, and maintaining a culture or civilization) that dollars and casualties measure very imperfectly. But despite these difficulties, most of us in our ordinary lives can say that there are some outcomes we prefer to others and that we prefer those outcomes either a lot or by only a small margin. For our purposes here, we need only assume that we can say *which* outcomes are better than others; we do not have to assume that we can say *how much* better one is than another.

Applying these methods to an arms race, for example, the worst outcome usually is when the other side has a much more effective capability than one's own. This is especially true when the possibility of a credible first-strike capability is at issue. To be at the mercy of such a force is the sucker (*S*) outcome; to have it would be temptation (*T*). To reduce an arms race and so to be able to devote more resources to domestic needs is quite a good outcome—one of reward (*R*). In a highly competitive and ideologically charged situation, perhaps it is less desirable than being able to wipe out your opponent, but it is clearly better than the punishment (*P*) of a mutual arms race carried on at substantial expense.

Thus the payoff situation is just the same as for the hapless prisoners who are asked to confess. Given the conditions laid down for the prisoners' dilemma—that the relative payoffs are as described, that there is no communication, and that this is a one-time, single-play situation—the rational choice for each player acting alone is to take the temptation to defect. That assures him or her of the better outcome, whichever action the other takes. If the second player also defects, the first gets P, which is bad but, at least, better than S; if the second does not defect, then our first gets T, which is even better than R. There is no effective incentive to cooperate; hence, both prisoners will defect and both will end up with quite a bad outcome (P), though not the very worst that might have happened to either if one cooperated while the other defected (S).

THE SECURITY DILEMMA

Does this mean, because we have pictured the relative payoffs as in a prisoners' dilemma, that two nations in an arms race are condemned to the risk and waste of a never-ending, costly arms competition? In 1950 that seemed to be the case. President Truman's scientific advisers told him they could build a powerful new weapon, hundreds of times more powerful than the atomic bomb: This was to be the hydrogen bomb (the H-bomb). It would be an awesome weapon, and any war in which it was used surely would leave millions dead. Some Americans would have liked best to be sole owner of the new bomb (T) but would have settled for a situation where no country had it (R). But the Russians had all the same basic scientific knowledge that the Americans had, and neither power would consider allowing the other to have such a fearsome weapon unless it also had one. It seemed better to go ahead and build it if the Russians could be expected to build it also (P). Even though building an H-bomb would leave both countries exposed to its dangers, it seemed better than being at the mercy of the Russians without a counter (S). Lacking any prospect of an enforceable agreement that neither would build H-bombs, both sides felt themselves forced to build

a weapon that they might have preferred didn't exist. This is the essence of the security dilemma: One may lose greatly by failing to trust the other, but one risks losing even more if the trust proves misplaced.

Yet this is not always the outcome, for, unlike the prisoners, national governments sometimes find it possible to communicate and to commit themselves to cooperate. A formal agreement, perhaps a treaty, if combined with inspection to verify whether the agreement is being kept, provides the instrument for commitment. It takes a long time to build and deploy enough modern weapons to be militarily decisive—unlike the act of defection in prison, which requires only a moment. With good inspection techniques, one nation can expect to detect betrayal before it becomes effective; thus, at worst, it would end up with a P payoff rather than with an S. That inspection may be agreed on and mutually executed (with inspectors permitted to roam about each others' countries) or merely unilaterally carried out by mutually tolerated means (observation satellites and, perhaps, spies). But only if each has reliable information about the other's activities—and knows that the other has information—can they make and keep a commitment.

Not all arms-race situations fit the prisoners'-dilemma model, though communication is still a critical element in any effort to cooperate. The previous example assumed that a situation of strategic parity offered a reasonably good solution—the second best of four for each of the two parties. Probably a different situation applied to the American–Soviet rivalry during the 1950s and, perhaps, the early 1960s. The Russians were in a position of strategic inferiority; they could not credibly threaten to make war against the United States except in response to the most dire threat to their interests in Eastern Europe. Although they had the military means to deter any unprovoked American attack, they dared not do anything that might endanger the American global position so that the U.S. government would be tempted to use nuclear weapons.

For the Russians, the payoffs may well have stayed like those of the prisoners' dilemma. But this was not the way the Americans saw things. The temptation (T), of spending heavily to

widen American superiority had less attraction for them because it promised to be so expensive and offered few real gains. They were satisfied with the status quo of the existing arms balance (*R*). A reversal of American superiority (*S*) was, of course, least preferred but highly unlikely given the American ability to keep track of Russian armaments by means of space satellite photography and overflights by U-2 planes. (Officials in the American executive branch with access to secret information from these sources did not share the worries of others about the so-called missile gap.) With this information and the wealth and scientific resources of the American economy, the United States did not see Soviet dominance as a real threat.

The Arms Race in the 1960s

		Soviet Union	
		Limit arms	Race harder
United States	Limit arms	*1, 2 (R, R)*	*4, 1 (S, T)*
	Race harder	*2, 4 (T, S)*	*3, 3 (P, P)*

Because the Americans preferred the rewards of cooperation to the costs of trying to widen or even fully maintain their own superiority, the situation was no longer strictly one of prisoners' dilemma. Nevertheless, the Americans were quite prepared, as second best, to punish the Russians (and of course themselves) if Moscow refused to cooperate. The two countries could reach a cooperative solution *if* the Americans could show that (1) they were fully aware of Russian missile-building efforts, so the Russians could not push the *S* outcome on them without their knowledge, and (2) the American payoffs were indeed as described—that is, America was prepared to go to great lengths to match new Russian missile building with enough of its own so as not to fall behind. The Americans also had to be able to show that (3) their political system was strong enough to undertake such a project (that is, that American taxpayers would support it with very high expenditures) and that (4) their economy was strong enough to carry the burden.

Ultimately, of course, the Russians did catch up, in effect because the Americans permitted them to do so. Why? By the mid 1960s the relative number of weapons on both sides meant far less than it had; even with numerical inferiority the Russians were strong enough to provide certain retaliation at a level of damage that could readily discourage any American attack. Under those circumstances, it made little difference whether the Russians had only a third of the American number of missiles or as many. At least it no longer made enough difference to make worthwhile the great new American expenditures required to restore the old ratio. The situation changed, and a new set of outcomes was accepted, because American perception of the payoffs changed even further from that of a prisoners' dilemma. For the United States, S became a much more acceptable result, really no worse than P (provided that the outcome of S was parity, not a reversal of superiority in favor of the Russians, as many began to fear by the 1980s).

A very important way in which undesirable outcomes for both players may be avoided, therefore, is through changes in the payoff table. This often occurs because of technological or economic developments that make formerly preferred outcomes more costly or more difficult to achieve. In this case, it became almost impossible to achieve an advantage in strategic weapons that would lead to any real military or political advantage. There was also some shift in values, and many people in America—particularly out of fatigue with the Vietnam War—decided that a military advantage as compared with settling for parity was just not especially desirable. Also, note the importance of technological change in facilitating communication: Observation satellites and aircraft made it possible for each side to check immediately on whether the other was building its capabilities too fast.

PROMOTING COOPERATION

Confrontations between the same parties occur repeatedly in international politics. When that happens, each country's ac-

tions in any single round of the game have consequences not only for the payoffs specified in that round, but for those of other, later situations as well. It is a logical next step, then, to consider what happens when a prisoners'-dilemma situation occurs within what the participants think will be a string of relationships. Many experimental psychologists and other experts, including Anatol Rapoport and his colleagues, have examined situations like this under laboratory conditions. Their experience now includes thousands of players, with from fifty to several hundred plays by the same individuals. There is a typical sequence that many players adopt:

At the beginning they often play cooperatively, with each partner being rewarded. After a short while, however, one partner becomes tempted to defect. His partner will usually retaliate after being betrayed once or twice, so both take the punishment outcome. Each may thereafter try to reestablish cooperation, but, without means for overt communication, it is a difficult business, and a would-be cooperator may well continue to receive the sucker's penalty. He may interpret this as betrayal and so return to defection.

In international politics, too, it may be very hard to shift into cooperative behavior. The first initiatives may not be seen as cooperation at all, or, if perceived as such, they may be interpreted as weakness and thus be exploited. After a good deal of trial and error, however, many players do in fact succeed in cooperating consistently again, but it may be a long, painful time before a favorable pattern is established.

Under these conditions, each play is eventually seen not as an end in itself but as a means of communicating one's intentions to the other with the hope of promoting joint cooperation on later plays. In this way it resembles the ongoing politics among nations, where cooperation does breed expectations of cooperation and defection breeds continuing fears of double-crossing. Ultimately, over many plays, it does become possible to develop trust. After a while the players become increasingly confident that they know how each other will behave.

Among nation-states as well, each may observe an agreement (such as an arms-control treaty), even when in the immediate

short run it might seem in its interest to defect from the agree-ment—and each may observe it for deep reasons of self-interest that have nothing to do with ethics or morality. International law is, of course, violated frequently, but in normal day-to-day procedure (such as that concerning transportation, communi-cation, respect for the persons of ambassadors, and movement of travelers between nations), governments far more often ob-serve the accepted legal principles. Especially if their acts can easily be observed by others (again, ties for handling commu-nication and information between nations are crucial), they pass up the immediate benefits of seizing a valuable cargo or person because they cannot afford the reprisals and disruption of future traffic that would surely follow. Under such circumstances, it becomes in the Russians' interest to observe an agreement; we trust them only to serve that interest, not to be honest or moral.

Conditions to Encourage Cooperation

Other circumstances have been found to affect the frequency with which players, under experimental conditions, choose co-operative rather than competitive strategies. (These and other relevant findings are regularly reported in several journals: *Be-havioral Science; Journal of Conflict Resolution; Simulation and Games;* and *International Journal of Game Theory.*) We can then suggest their possible relevance for international politics. Of course, it is a long jump from the laboratory to the world of national leaders, and yet these experiments are intriguing. They are im-portant, too, because of an inherent limit in any analysis of the real world of international politics. We can only examine what has been done; if we want to generate preferred futures, we will have to look at behavior under other conditions and try to make analogies where appropriate.

1. Experimental evidence clearly supports the point made earlier that competitive strategies are more common where there is no means for the players to communicate with each other. Many kinds of information need to be communicated; activities, reasons for those activities, intentions, and preferences (payoff

structures) matter in varying degrees. Formal government-to-government communication facilities are a key part of this, but so are trade and various person-to-person contacts, such as tourism and cultural exchange.

2. When players do communicate, it seems essential that the communication be honest. If one player uses the opportunity to deceive the other, the result is often a longer run of mutual defection and double-crossing than happens when no communication is permitted.[2] President Carter's decision to impose economic sanctions on the Soviet Union for its invasion of Afghanistan stemmed partly from anger that Brezhnev had lied to him. Apparently, Brezhnev had told Carter that Afghanistan leader Hafizullah Amin had "requested the assistance" of Soviet troops— troops who then supervised Amin's deposition and assassination.

3. Competitive strategies are more common when the first player can reverse a decision about a particular play even after the decision has been made and communicated to the second player. When it is possible to change one's mind on seeing the other person's choice, it seems much more common for players to change a previously announced noncooperative act to a cooperative one in response to the other's cooperation than for players to switch a cooperative choice to betrayal so as to exploit the opportunity.

4. Competitive strategies nevertheless seem more common under circumstances where players' decisions are made consecutively (without a change to reverse them) than where both players communicate their decisions at the same time. This is probably because the player who has to move first often hesitates to expose himself to the sucker's penalty by leading with a cooperative play.

5. Some of these principles have been applied to a strategy proposed by social psychologist Charles Osgood, who calls his strategy "Gradual and Reciprocated Initiatives in Tension-reduction," or GRIT. He says one side should make some limited conciliatory gestures unilaterally (such as not building, or perhaps abandoning, some weapon), communicate the fact to the other side, and then look for some similar move by the other in return. If the other side seems to be taking advantage of your

apparent weakness by escalating, then you retaliate with a step carefully matched to the other side's escalation. You may later try other conciliatory gestures. By this strategy, actions may start off as unilateral, but they are limited and will only continue if the other side responds favorably.[3]

6. It helps to have some experience in doing things together to gain some common reward. A famous "robbers' cave" experiment, performed by several psychologists in a boys' camp, supports this point. The leaders divided the boys into two rival groups and deliberately encouraged rivalry between the groups. After the two groups had become quite hostile, the leaders then tried to see how the tensions might be reduced. They tried bringing the groups together for enjoyable events, but that did little good. Then they created situations where the two groups had to cooperate with each other in order to obtain something they both wanted. After reluctantly taking part in the latter activities, the boys eventually developed a new spirit, and antagonisms eased.

For international politics, this experiment suggests the importance of major cooperative action by hostile governments, an importance that goes far beyond the immediate goal the governments may try to reach. Joint activities in space might have some long-term effects in encouraging broader cooperation; so might joint activities to control global pollution. Long-term efforts to explore ways to develop trust and avoid the prisoners' dilemma might generate some mutual identification in addition to bringing the specific benefits of whatever concrete steps were undertaken.[4]

7. It makes a difference how the experimenter describes the game to the players before they begin. He can present it as: (1) a situation where the aim is for each player to do the best he can regardless of what happens to the other players; (2) a game where the aim is to do better than the other; or (3) a game where the important thing is for both to do well. Not surprisingly, people cooperate least often when the experimenter emphasizes "do better than the other" in the pregame orientation. The game description becomes a self-fulfilling prophecy. By analogy, it may very much matter what preconceptions people bring to the anal-

ysis of international politics. Those who have been taught—informally or in school—to think of the world as "red in tooth and claw" (where the overriding goal is to maximize the national interest of one's own state over all others) will be less ready to cooperate when they come to choose policies. What should be non-zero-sum situations may be interpreted so that the players' only concern is to maximize their relative well-being (or misery).

Professor Robert Axelrod conducted a tournament among 13 social scientists to see whose computerized stratgey for playing repeated prisoners' dilemma games would be most successful. Of all the strategies played, he found that tit for tat (cooperating after the opponent cooperated, defecting after a defection) was most successful, especially when coupled with optimism (opening with a cooperative move) and being somewhat forgiving (punishing once, then trying again to cooperate). But in analyzing the results carefully, he found that being somewhat *more* forgiving would have been even more successful; that is, all the social scientists played more competitively than would have been best.[5]

Thinking back on our prisoners in the police station, imagine how different their situation would have been if one or both of them had held some principle of "honor among thieves," with a prickly conscience that made it painful to betray the other. Suppose that both were in fact innocent—and moral people, at that. Each might well prefer to accept a long prison term rather than condemn the other unjustly to an even longer term. The payoffs thus would not coincide merely with jail terms. Under these circumstances (where the pangs of conscience associated with the temptation of defecting make *T* a very undesired outcome), they would actually get what would for them be the highest payoff when both refused to defect, and thus receive the very short jail sentence (*R*). In international politics, it is often easy to dismiss thoughts about the effect of morality, since not too many people are prepared to say "Better me dead than both of us" when considering deterrence of a country perceived as an enemy. But such considerations should not be ignored. Many Americans and Russians would at least hesitate to deliver

a nuclear first strike even if they thought they could do it with little cost to themselves in lives or dollars. President Kennedy is said to have refused military advisers' pleas to launch a surprise attack on the Cuban missile sites in part because he thought it would be wrong to do so.[6]

We must recognize from the beginning that international politics requires some mixture of conflict and cooperation. This is a fundamental restriction on excessively cold-blooded strategic thinking about cold war problems. One side alone cannot make all conflicts go away; yet, if we insist on seeing the world as a constant struggle, we will indeed make it more nearly so.

President John Kennedy meeting with the EXCOM during the Cuban missile crisis in October, 1962. (Courtesy of John F. Kennedy Library.)

6

Deterrence and Crisis Stability

Think, too, of the great part that is played by the unpredictable in war: think of it now, before you are actually committed to war. The longer a war lasts, the more things tend to depend on accidents. Neither you nor we can see into them: we have to abide their outcome in the dark. And when people are entering upon a war they do things the wrong way round. Action comes first, and it is only when they have already suffered that they begin to think.

Thucydides, *The Peloponnesian War*

THE PRISONERS' DILEMMA AGAIN

We must now move from the year-to-year competition of the arms race to consider the theory of deterrence and how it may work in a crisis. We shall begin by discussing the "normal" situation of deterrence through "balance of terror," using the kind of presentation developed in Chapter 5 for the prisoners' dilemma. The true prisoners' dilemma is probably not a common situation in international politics. However, under some circumstances there are grave risks that a previously safe non-zero-sum situation may turn into a dangerous form of prisoners' dilemma. Nuclear deterrence always carries this risk to some degree.

The following table represents the relative values that the U.S. and Soviet governments might attach to the use of nuclear weapons in a typical noncrisis situation.

Noncrisis Decisions About Using Nuclear Weapons

| | | Soviet Union | |
		Wait	Attack
United	Wait	1, 1 (R, R)	4, 2 (S, T)
States	Attack	2, 4 (T, S)	3, 3 (P, P)

For both participants, the best outcome is where both wait—that is, where peace is preserved. Under the best of conditions, war would leave both parties much worse off than at present. Given the capabilities of each side to retaliate, the first strike is a very unattractive course of action.

Remember that, in the prisoners' dilemma, one is better off defecting (or attacking) whether the other side defects or cooperates. In this example, however, while each is better off attacking if the other intends to attack, each is also clearly better off waiting if the other also waits. Since the payoff from peace (R) greatly exceeds the temptation to hit first (T), this is no prisoners' dilemma. Neither side will attack, and peace will be preserved. This is essentially—in abstract form—what a situation of stable deterrence looks like. It was also the condition of the world for most of the last three decades.

Yet a policy of restraint is acceptable only as long as neither side has a first-strike capability and as long as each side retains some confidence that the other also sees a first strike as poor policy. Stability can be shaken by a number of possible developments. A great technological breakthrough for one side, such as an extremely effective ABM and air-defense system and superaccurate MIRVs, might raise the gains from a first strike (T); that is, it might reduce the damage to be expected from the opponent's retaliation. Even the information—correct or mistaken—that the enemy was about to achieve such a breakthrough might suddenly change the estimates of the power receiving the information. If the enemy seems about to gain the ability to attack you, a preemptive attack might seem the rational thing to do.

DETERRENCE AND CRISIS INSTABILITY

Technological change alone is unlikely to make much difference in deterrence stability as long as both superpowers maintain heavy research and development programs and keep a varied set of strategic weapons (SLBMs, manned bombers, and, perhaps, land-based ICBMs), so a single technical breakthrough by one side cannot be decisive. But a much more plausible set of events leading to upset of a deterrent balance can be imagined in a crisis—perhaps one such as the Cuban missile crisis of 1962, with some moderate variations. This would happen if one power violated a principle later laid down by Henry Kissinger:

> If crisis management requires cold and even brutal measures to show determination, it also imposes the need to show opponents a way out. Grandstanding is good for the ego but bad for foreign policy. Many wars have started because no line of retreat was left open. Superpowers have a special obligation not to humiliate each other.[1]

As it happened, in 1962 President Kennedy was careful to give Khrushchev an opportunity to withdraw the Russian missiles with some dignity and face. He termed the outcome a victory for peace, not a victory for the United States. But suppose he had dramatized the situation as an impending American victory and a great loss of prestige for the Russians; and suppose he had claimed that it proved the Russians were unable to deter any serious American pressure against the Communist world and he had followed up with efforts to overthrow the Castro government. Under these circumstances, the value of peace (R) to the Russians—and especially for the humiliated Khrushchev, who would have faced immediate ouster as leader of the USSR—would have dropped sharply; the stability of the whole Communist system might have been at risk. At the same time, Khrushchev might have read Kennedy's actions as indicating that the Americans had much greater confidence in their first-strike capability than he had previously thought. That might have led the Russians to raise substantially their estimates of the damage the Americans could inflict (S) and of the likelihood

of an American attack. Thus, even though a Russian first strike would still have looked like a bad outcome to the Russians (T is unchanged), using even a moderate first-strike capability might have looked better to the Soviet Union than continuing to live with the Americans after a bad diplomatic or military defeat. Whether the Americans would have attacked or waited, the situation would have become a prisoners' dilemma, and attacking the United States would have been the better of each pair of generally bad outcomes for the Soviet Union.

Possible Crisis Options for the Soviet Union

| | | Soviet Union | |
		Wait	Attack
United	Wait	2(R)	1(T)
States	Attack	4(S)	3(P)

We might even suppose that President Kennedy, who in our imaginary scenario acted rashly and claimed a victory over the Russians, then thought the matter over more calmly and realized the risks he was running. Conceivably, he might have decided that he had in fact tipped the balance toward a Russian preemptive attack and then felt required to preempt the preemption! The point is that, in the course of a crisis, previously stable estimates can change suddenly and sharply.

The scenarios just sketched may seem improbable, but they are not. President Kennedy is reported to have said at the time of the Cuban missile crisis that he thought the chances of nuclear war were about one in three. Perhaps he was mistaken, though in a very real sense such a situation can become a self-fulfilling prophecy. Thinking war is near can bring it near through pressures for preemption, just as thinking war is near can also bring greater efforts to avoid disaster. The problem is especially serious, given how fallible human leaders are and how easily they can misperceive each other's intentions—especially under the enormous pressures of a nuclear crisis. The problem will

become clear if we now look at some of the assumptions about decision making that were implicit in the previous discussion but that are not necessarily correct.

Assuming There Is Only a Single Event

In a real crisis, decision makers must consider not just what is happening now but what has happened in the past and, especially, what may happen in the future. If I behave reasonably now, will my opponent take that as a sign to moderate his or her demands in the future, or, to the contrary, will my opponent see my reasonableness as a sign of weakness, to be exploited by still greater demands in the future? Will my allies, as well as my enemies, interpret this as an unwillingness to take risks to defend them? The specter of British Prime Minister Chamberlain's effort to appease Hitler at Munich in 1938 remains to haunt contemporary leaders. We noted this kind of consideration in our earlier discussion about repeated plays of prisoners' dilemma. Leaders must worry about their states' reputation for resolve and for being a reliable ally and about their ability to make credible deterrent threats and commitments. (An argument for continuing the Vietnam War, despite the ghastly struggle it had become, was that America must be seen by her allies as honoring her commitment.)

After repeated losses or defeats, decision makers' assessments of the value of different outcomes are likely to shift. Facing the prospect of large losses from a military or political effort that has gone bad, the decision maker may imagine that one more effort has a better chance of winning, recouping what would otherwise be humiliating losses. In such situations, we may speak of throwing good money after bad or irrationally shooting the works.

Assuming Both Sides Have the Same Values

To simplify matters, we assumed that both parties had the same valuation of the various outcomes for themselves. This, of course, is not necessarily true. A status quo power will value peace more

than will leaders who feel their country has been deprived of a place in the sun. Russians will have somewhat different values than Americans; Communists will have different values than capitalists.

Assuming Countries Are Single Decision Makers

In a real crisis, not just one but several decision makers will be involved on each side, each giving advice and having some direct control over the outcomes. Each will be concerned with his or her own personal and organizational interests as well as with his or her perception of the national interest. As shown in Chapter 4, those perceptions may differ drastically, and it matters greatly how those various perceptions and interests are put together in arriving at a final decision.

Even the President is subject to such considerations. Political leaders rarely expect to be in office indefinitely and are likely to worry about being returned to office in the next election. The temptation political leaders feel to take short-term gains or avoid short-term losses, even at the cost of greater long-term costs to the country at large, may be very strong, especially if the general public does not understand how likely those long-term losses are. Political leaders care, in a way others do not, about preserving their own power now, and they may rationalize this with the view that it is really in the country's best interest for them to stay in office.

In the Cuban missile crisis, President Kennedy felt that any display of weakness was likely to damage his party badly in the congressional elections only a month away. If, on the other hand, he had seen the American people as very "dovish," Kennedy might have grasped at "peace in our time," even at the risk of later war. In any case, different decision makers will evaluate outcomes differently and will have different attitudes toward risk taking. It matters who is making the decisions—Chamberlain or Churchill, Hitler or Helmut Schmidt. Extremely deviant individuals rarely get to the top leadership positions in large, bureaucratic systems in industrialized societies, but less dramatic individual differences still can matter. Richard Nixon, un-

der the strains of his final days in the presidency, is said to have sobbed, beaten his fists on the floor of his office, and to have mused about his ability to release the forces of nuclear disaster. Defense Secretary Schlesinger took special precautions to prevent unauthorized military acts or irrational orders. Had there really been an international crisis at that time, Nixon's decisions would not necessarily have been the same as those of another President or even those recommended by his advisers.

Being a member of a small group can very strongly affect both the perceptions and the behavior of an individual. Pressures build on the individual to conform to the view of the group and not to challenge the group. In this process, the perceptions of the individual may be altered. Laboratory experiments by psychologists demonstrate the conforming pressures that a small group can have on its members. One experiment had a group of six to eight people comparing visual stimuli—the length of two lines, for example. However, only one member of the group was actually being observed; the others (unknown to the "naive subject") had been instructed to give false answers. The subject then heard the others in this small group saying that the shorter line was longer, the smaller cube larger, and so on. At first, the subject acted puzzled and upset, but then he began to conform and to describe the stimuli as described by the others! The naive subject began to say that the short line was longer and the smaller cube larger, even though his eyes were looking at a clearly shorter line or smaller cube.[2]

One version of the individual's conformity to small group views is what Irving Janis calls "groupthink." Janis looked at a number of American foreign-policy decisions, including the Bay of Pigs invasion in 1961, the response to the North Korean invasion of the South in 1950, the decision to set up the Marshall Plan, the decisions to escalate the war in Vietnam, decisions made about Pearl Harbor prior to the attack, and the Cuban missile crisis of 1962. Janis sums up his central theme as follows: "The more amiability and esprit de corps among the members of a policy-making in-group, the greater is the danger that independent critical thinking will be replaced with groupthink,

which is likely to result in irrational and dehumanizing actions directed against out-groups."[3]

Janis comes up with a number of major symptoms of group-think. In terms of self-image, a close and amiable group will produce an "illusion of invulnerability." This feeling and view of one's group is overly optimistic and encourages risks. Other research has identified the phenomenon of the "risky shift": Individuals respond to real and hypothetical situations in a more conservative way when by themselves than when in a group; for a variety of reasons, they are willing to engage in riskier behavior when responding to the same situations in a group setting.

A second symptom, the group's unquestioned belief in its own morality, also involves self-images. The group setting leads the individual members to feel that this group couldn't be any-thing but good (". . . and we all agree on that, don't we?"). This symptom will lead group members to ignore the ethical or moral consequences of their decisions. The assumption is that the group is moral, and therefore the decisions of the group will be moral. The third symptom is a stereotyped view of the opponent's leadership as being too evil or stupid to be negotiated with on a good-faith basis.

The groupthink process, then, leads to a shared illusion of unanimity. Groupthink leads to efforts to rationalize the group's decisions, to justify them no matter what they might be. This helps to screen out any warnings or counterinformation that might lead the group to reconsider. Groupthink also leads to direct pressure on any individual who argues against the ster-eotypes that the group produces; it leads to self-censorship of doubts and counterarguments (much as does the perception experiment described on page 121).

The conditions that promote groupthink stem from group co-hesiveness. The group is more likely to stick together if it is isolated from outsiders and outside views as well as from in-formation that might challenge the images of the group. Finally, the appearance of a group leader who promotes a preferred solution is another major influence on groupthink. It is not nec-essary for the others in the group to be mere toadies or yes-

men for this sort of effect to take place: Most people want a leader to be decisive, within limits; others in the group will go along with the leader because they believe the leader shares their own values or because the leader controls promotion decisions.

A good example of this is the American decision to send military aid to South Korea immediately upon hearing of the North Korean attack. President Truman walked into the meeting of his advisers and gave approval to the plan to be presented by Secretary of State Acheson. The rest of the discussion was based on that view rather than on any other. Indeed, one of the reasons so little groupthink occurred during the Cuban crisis was because President Kennedy consciously removed himself from a number of the sessions of the group so that his presence would not inhibit the broadest possible review of alternative options and views (an interesting mixture of the intellectual and social processes at work). Groupthink was avoided also because participants were supposed to act as generalists, *not* to represent particular roles. They were also supposed to be as skeptical and challenging as possible in a very informal atmosphere with no formal agenda or rules of protocol.

Assuming Leaders Have Only Two Choices

In a real crisis, a decision maker has to choose not simply between two options—attack and no attack—but among a wider set of options. If he or she looks carefully, those options will range widely on a scale from nearly pure cooperation to nearly pure competition. No leaders can hope to consider all possible alternatives, for under the best of circumstances they must choose within a fairly short time span and cannot think of everything. The quality and scope of a search for different options and the definition of the problem vary for different decision makers and different organizational constraints. Still, the marks of a good political decision maker include the ability both to consider a wide range of possible options and to make a good initial choice of which options to look at carefully. The options called to mind are not picked at random out of the air but reflect established

search procedures. A good chess player is not just one who chooses well among a given set of options but one who knows how to pick from the nearly infinite number of available strategies the most promising ones for careful consideration in the first place. For instance, in the early stages of the Cuban missile crisis, President Kennedy's advisers quickly converged on a choice of two options—a "surgical" air strike against the Soviet missile emplacements or a landing in Cuba by American troops. Kennedy disliked the implications of both choices and insisted that his advisers come up with something else, which ultimately became the blockade. Kennedy's degree of independence in rejecting the options offered by his advisers and insisting that they find another is unusual in decision makers acting under the time pressures of a crisis.

Assuming Leaders See Clearly

In order for decision makers to act at all in a complex world of far more information (and misinformation) than they can handle, they must use various perceptual screens. Misperception means that decision makers' images of reality are screening out important signals in some way—ignoring them completely, interpreting them incorrectly, or changing the information to fit existing images. People try to achieve cognitive consistency; that is, they try to keep the images they hold from clashing with or contradicting each other. Sometimes new information forces an image to change so that it will then contradict other images. This often happens when information arrives to correct an initially bad image of a group of people or of an enemy. Rather than change one's perception of the opponent's capabilities or intentions, a person may simply ignore or reshape the new information. For example, John Foster Dulles, Secretary of State under Eisenhower, saw the Soviet Union as implacably hostile. Increases in Soviet armed forces of course, showed this hostility; cuts in the size of Soviet armed forces merely indicated, to Dulles, economic weakness rather than a possible decrease in hostility.[4]

The use of historical analogies, though often imperfect, will lead to selective perception, that is, the tendency to look for

similarities between a present episode and past ones while ignoring the important differences. One of the most famous examples of this mechanism is the "Munich syndrome." Decision
makers in the United States and Britain who were active during
the 1930s when the western democracies attempted to appease
Hitler (of which the Munich agreement was the main symbol)
tended to use this event as an analogy for many postwar events
that only partially resembled it. The Suez crisis of 1956 was
driven in part by the selective perceptions of British Prime Minister Anthony Eden, who saw Egypt's Nasser as another Hitler
and thus someone who could not be appeased. The historical
analogy, in order to fit the current case, required selecting certain aspects of the situation and utterly ignoring others.

Related to this is the process of wishful thinking, that is, the
influence of fears and desires on perception. We often see either
what we fear or what we wish to be the case. A study of the
chief European decision makers in the period immediately preceding World War I found that the Kaiser feared England, which
had been ruled until shortly before then by an uncle whom he
also feared. The Kaiser also, it seems, perceived as real the events
he was afraid would come true. Simply hearing that the British
felt they still had freedom of action caused the Kaiser to write:
"The net has been suddenly thrown over our heads and England sneeringly reaps the most brilliant success of her persis-
tently prosecuted anti-German world policy . . . ." Similarly,
leaders who wished to see peace thought they saw it when
Chamberlain returned to Britain from Munich exulting that there
was "peace in our time." The strong desire for peace led many
followers of Chamberlain to see carving up Czechoslovakia as
the act that would placate Hitler and save the peace, while there
was really no evidence at all that this would happen.

Foreign-policy decision makers often underestimate how un-
clear a message or speech may be to someone else, in spite of
the sender's efforts to make the message clear. They assume
that others will understand their actions and behavior much
more easily than is the case.

Once we see others as opponents or enemies, the opponent
labeled "enemy" takes on certain characteristics—and we then

behave toward that enemy in certain ways. *Defense mechanisms* protect the individual from things that would otherwise make him or her uncomfortable and anxious. One defense process is *projection,* where we project onto others feelings, characteristics, and desires we cannot admit exist in ourselves.

A major factor in projection is the existence of something acting as a scapegoat, that is, as an excuse for failings that we cannot admit to having. An enemy becomes a scapegoat when we accuse the enemy of the things we dislike in ourselves. The accusation is used to justify our own behavior, which may be similar to that of the opponent. In foreign relations, we often see our enemy as aggressive and seeking dominance and conquest—as a state capable of evil and brutality. Being able to crusade against such an enemy allows us to have the satisfaction of believing in our own moral superiority, of having a cause and being needed by that cause to oppose and defeat the enemy. We can then hate and kill without being bothered by our consciences. Having an enemy leads us to see the world in simplistic black-and-white images—clearcut distinctions of good and evil, of "us" versus "them."

The enemy image also distorts the view of the opponent. By seeing the opponent as evil, we lose the ability to see the world as the opponent might see it. This gives us only a very incomplete view of a situation—and a dangerous one at that—by blinding us to how our "virtuous" behavior may appear to the other party and how it may worsen a situation. In addition, seeing the opponent as an enemy often leads us to screen out or misinterpret any conciliatory, cooperative, or tension-reducing behavior of the opponent. This tendency may result in ignoring chances to stop a war before it starts or to end a war already begun.

A major study of the period immediately preceding the outbreak of World War I indicated that the decision makers of each state perceived threats of hostile behavior and that these perceptions led to hostile behavior toward hostile states. In other words, other states were seen as enemies if they were in opposing military alliances and had engaged in arms races and competition for colonies; they were then perceived as behaving

in a hostile manner (whether they were actually doing so or not), and this hostility was then matched by the perceiver's hostility. This type of process is known as a conflict spiral, which can escalate a minor incident—or, indeed, one that might not even have happened—into a major war.

When such images are held by each side in a conflict, there is said to be a mirror-image situation. Each side sees the same things, but in reverse; each sees the other as an enemy or a devil, and each sees itself as moral, virile, and so on. The cold war has been studied using chronologies of U.S.–Soviet foreign-policy events. The results indicated an exact mirror-image model. Both the United States and the Soviet Union showed the same pattern: "I am a 'consolidationist' [a state that seeks only to preserve what it has and not to expand]; *he knows* that I am consolidationist; but, *he* is an expansionist."[5] As with the conflict spiral, a mirror image such as this may keep a conflict going for long periods of time and make it that much more difficult to end. This kind of thinking is well described by George Kennan:

> I have heard it argued: "Oh, well, they [the Soviets] know we [the U.S.] have no aggressive intentions. They know we have no idea of using these arms for an attack on them." To this there are two things to be said. When one attempts to explain to people in the Pentagon and to like-minded civilians that perhaps the Russians are not really eager to attack the West—that they have very good reasons for not planning or wishing to do anything of that sort, one is met with the reply: "Ah, yes, but look at the size of their armaments, and concede that in matters of this sort we cannot be bothered to take into account their intentions—intentions are too uncertain and too hard to determine; we can take into account only capabilities; we must assume the Russians to be desirous, that is, of doing anything bad to us that their capabilities would permit them to do." Now is it our view that *we* should take account only of *their capabilities,* disregarding *their intentions,* but we should expect them to take account only of *our* supposed *intentions,* disregarding our *capabilities?* . . . If we are going to disregard everything but their capabilities, we cannot simultaneously expect them to disregard everything but our intentions.[6]

Focusing on Threats, Especially Military Threats

To the degree that military considerations are important, military leaders will be involved in the decision. Both they and political decision makers may overemphasize the role of military instruments in solving the problem. People writing about international politics often concentrate too heavily on military means, on conflicting rather than cooperative acts, and on threats or punishments rather than on inducements or rewards. In fact, the majority of peacetime acts directed by states at one another—even between opponents—are cooperative or neutral, not conflictful. Severe threats or punishments may arouse great fear and stress in decision makers and may interfere with their ability to make accurate assessments of others' capabilities or intentions or even of the value of various outcomes to themselves. By arousing irrational responses, threats may be counterproductive.

Assuming Decision Making Is Not Made Under Stress

A crisis differs from a normal decision-making situation in that a crisis arises with little warning, provides relatively little time for decision, and poses a high threat to decision makers and their states. Crisis behavior is behavior under stress. It is difficult to understand other people's motives and behavior under the best of circumstances and more difficult in crosscultural assessments, where capitalist Americans may have to try to think like Communist Russians or Chinese. It becomes even more difficult in times of crisis. We know that behavior in crisis typically is different from what people would do under normal conditions. The rational person in the prisoners' dilemma has a hard time at best. We nevertheless assumed that he was able to perceive his options clearly, to consider calmly the likely actions of his opposite number, and to weigh carefully the values he attached to possible outcomes. But in a crisis, this is precisely what may not happen.

Because the crisis brings a major threat to something held dear, the decision maker probably will try to gather a great deal

of information to help make a rational decision. Yet he or she has little time to consider all that information. Modern governments can swamp a decision maker in intelligence material. A crisis may be a period of information overload, with messages and advice coming in from observers on the spot, from aides who have been asked to find out what is happening, from ambassadors, and from many others. Overload forces the decision maker to make some arbitrary choices about what to consider—a major form of screening. Psychological processes set those screens; they may distort one's view of the world and reduce ability to interpret and weigh the quality of information. Overload may obscure true "signals" by hiding them in "noise." This was the case of Pearl Harbor, where, among other things, having broken the Japanese code, the Americans were able to read *all* of the Japanese messages. Instead of helping, all this information just swamped the American intelligence bureaucracy. The Allies' strategy regarding the location of the World War II D-day landings in Europe was consciously similar—to overload the Germans with a great deal of information, much of it pure noise in the form of false signals. In this way, they hoped that the Germans would wrongly calculate the invasion site, which was exactly what happened.

A threat implies fear and stress. Under small or moderate amounts of stress, individuals may intensify their efforts to examine their options, search widely for better options, and choose carefully among them. Stress may make us work harder and more effectively if we believe there is a chance of finding a satisfactory policy, if we have time enough to consider options, and if we have the resources to devise and carry out such a policy.

Laboratory experiments and studies of real decision makers in World War I, the Korean War, and the Cuban crisis have indicated the following effects of stress on perception:

1. During the crisis, *communications tended to become shorter and more stereotyped* as stress increased. Stereotypes not only distort,

they tend to break things into black-and-white images and foster the creation and continuation of the "image of the enemy."

2. Not surprisingly, then, crisis also can lead to an *overperception of the level of hostility* and violence in the behavior of one's opponents—in other words, seeing hostility where it might not exist (wishful thinking or the self-fulfilling prophecy). On the other hand, one *underperceives the hostility and violence in one's own actions.* In addition, if a state sees itself as the object of another's hostility, it will express hostility to that state.

3. With this process, we are back in a *conflict spiral*—a mirror-image situation between two states that perceive each other as enemies. *Perceptions of anxiety or fear* are likely to increase in these conditions. As they do, they might lead decision makers to *ignore perceptions of capabilities.* The desire to break the tension through any end to the crisis—even war—could lead to ignoring the strength or weakness of oneself, one's allies, and one's opponents. This luckily did not happen in the Cuban crisis. Neither Kennedy nor Khrushchev called nuclear weapons "paper tigers" (as the Chinese did in the period before they acquired them), nor did they underplay the destructiveness of such weapons. Each went out of his way to stress the consequences of their use.

4. As the crisis grows, decision makers increasingly feel that their *own range of alternatives becomes more restricted.* The crisis, therefore, cuts down their perceptions of available alternatives. At the same time, decision makers see the *alternatives of their opponents as expanding.* "While we will have no choice but to go to war, they could avoid war by doing any of a number of things."

5. High stress is likely to bring procrastination, shifting of responsibility to others, and *"bolstering,"* that is, an exaggeration of favorable consequences and minimization of unfavorable ones.

6. Highly stressed decision makers may react fatalistically to their predicaments and become more prone to anger and despair. In 1914, for instance, some tired, tense, overworked leaders simply stopped searching for further ways to escape war, even though they certainly did not want it. It could happen again.[7]

AVOIDING THE ESCALATION OF CRISES

There are a number of paths by which nuclear war between the superpowers might erupt. Table 6-1 lists the most important possibilities. The last two are the least likely: Terrorist or third-party use of nuclear weapons certainly is not implausible, but it probably could be accurately identified and not be blamed on a superpower; technical improvements make the explosion of a nuclear weapon by physical accident quite improbable. The other possibilities, however, are very real.

Continued avoidance of nuclear war over decades of confrontation will require a number of steps taken by policymakers with the support of their citizens. Among these steps are:

1. Very careful, calm statesmanship, with attention to developing standard operating procedures that minimize stress, maximize the search for alternatives, and control the distortions of judgment that can arise from group decision making and organizational politics.

2. The building of a sense of predictability, identity, and mutual interest among top decision makers and, perhaps even more importantly, among those members of the elite and the attentive public below the top decision makers, whose support would be needed for policies of restraint. Predictability is essential, be-

Table 6-1
How a Nuclear War Might Begin in a Crisis

Deliberate escalation by top leaders in the face of military or political losses.

Preemption by top leaders in anticipation of an enemy's deliberate escalation.

False warning from misinterpreting enemy alert procedures.

Computer or human error in information systems.

Unauthorized firing by lower-level military officers, such as submarine commanders or field commanders in Europe.

"Catalytic" war begun by smaller nuclear power or terrorists.

Physical accident to warhead or delivery vehicle.

cause uncertainty about the other's probable behavior may lead to behavior aimed just at avoiding worst-case outcomes, even though such outcomes may be very improbable. Identity and mutual interest matter as a means of developing conscience that produces a beneficial shift in values and hence in the payoff structure. Here it is a matter of coming to see the other person's welfare as having an importance of its own. Conscience is usually most effective in governing our behavior toward those we know well. Narrowing the "human distance" is an effective way to discourage violence. Where the victims have no discernible characteristics or identity, or where people and suffering cannot be seen (as when a missile is sent across the globe), it is easier to give or obey orders to inflict pain. The ease with which very ordinary and normally moral people will inflict pain on a faceless victim has been illustrated by laboratory experiments.[8]

3. Deliberate efforts to build weapons systems that do not give an inordinate advantage to a first strike—perhaps even self-denial in not building weapons that might give a good first-strike capability.

4. Technological improvements to strengthen information processing, control, and the avoidance of human and mechanical error.

5. Arms control and disarmament steps, including efforts to share information that could assure the other side that no first strike is contemplated.

6. A good deal of luck.

Left: President Harry S. Truman. (Harry S. Truman Library/Magnum Photos, Inc.) *Right:* Burns on the body of a forty-five-year-old woman at Nagasaki. She died on October 15, 1945. Difficult questions about the morality of bombing civilians continue to trouble us. (Photograph by Masao Shiotsuki, from *Hiroshima and Nagasaki: The Physical, Medical, and Social Effects of the Atomic Bombings*, translated by Eisei Ishikawa and David L. Swain. Copyright © 1981 by Hiroshima City and Nagasaki City. Reprinted by permission of Basic Books, Inc., Publishers, New York.)

7

Restraints in War

[If someone were] to lose his little finger tomorrow he would not sleep tonight, but, provided he never saw them, he would snore with the most profound security over the ruin of a hundred million of his brethren.

Adam Smith, The Wealth of Nations

ETHICS AND WAR

In our discussion of arms races and deterrence, we have concentrated on such questions as the following: What has been the historic experience? What are some analytical perspectives that may help us understand these complex issues? What evidence is there to support assertions about the causes and consequences of arms races? Occasionally we have alluded to moral and ethical considerations as possible restraints on behavior, but that has been the extent of our discussion of ethics and morality. We have not gone to the further questions: Is morality merely a matter of beating the Communists by whatever means? What actions are moral or ethical? If a war did occur, what principles should guide our own behavior, or what principles would we want to guide the behavior of our leaders? In fact, the issue of limited war—especially limited nuclear war—not only raises questions about what *can* happen under various conditions, but

it raises crucial value-laden questions about what we would *want* to happen.

Moral or ethical propositions concern how people ought to behave rather than how people in fact do behave. Ethical reasoning is basically deductive reasoning—one starts with a few given principles and deduces from them a set of further propositions. While people often make ethical statements without proceeding carefully and logically, the same is also true about many empirical statements. When done carefully, ethical deductive reasoning can be fully as rigorous as mathematical or other formal reasoning.

We cannot completely ignore such issues in a book on deterrence and war. Instead, we shall discuss the historical tradition and background of discourse on the matter of limits to be observed in the course of warfare and consider how these might apply to modern nuclear war: Are there circumstances under which nuclear weapons should not be used? Are there targets that are not permissible by widely accepted ethical precepts? The purpose here is not to insist on answers but only to offer a discussion as a means of opening up such issues for consideration.

The Realist Position

At one end of the spectrum of ethical thought about warfare are the views that essentially say that war (or any act in war) is justifiable if it seems to serve the national interest, or that perhaps rightness depends solely on the ends being sought rather than on the methods used to obtain them. The first implies that if the populace as a whole desires something, leaders can and should seek to obtain it with whatever means are available. (We should nevertheless be wary of such attributions of preference to a whole aggregate of groups, interests, and classes.) This version of realism holds that, regardless of the moral restraints we may accept in interpersonal behavior, international politics is so anarchic—a war of each against all—that mere self-preservation requires the abandonment of moral inhibitions in the

world arena. For those who hold the second view, there are legitimate and illegitimate goals, but, provided that your intended goals or ends are "just," any means may be employed in world politics to reach them.

Many people may express such a viewpoint, but it is not clear how many really believe it is a guide to action. Most adults come to believe that the law is important, that it should be obeyed at least most of the time, and that if it is to be disobeyed, it should not be disobeyed lightly. Civil disobedience may be permissible, but only for some "higher" moral purpose.[1] International law is generally regarded as one of the least authoritative and effective forms of law, but even international law is given some respect and observance, and not solely from motives of self-interest. When occupying the Vietnam village of My Lai, Lieutenant William Calley deliberately ordered and supervised the killing of hundreds of innocent, noncombatant civilians. Conceivably, this action might have safeguarded a few American troops from Communist Vietcong guerrillas disguised as civilians (though this was a rather far-fetched excuse in the My Lai case). Nevertheless, Calley's act violated U.S. Army regulations, international law, and most people's moral sense of what was right and wrong. Calley was tried and convicted by an army court, though not punished severely.

Similarly, after World War II, many German and Japanese wartime leaders were tried by Allied military tribunals at Nürnberg and Tokyo. They were charged with the deliberate killing of civilians and prisoners of war and with "waging aggressive war." Some of these acts, such as killing prisoners of war, were clearly forbidden by international law through such enactments as the Geneva Convention. Others, such as waging aggressive war, were less clearly outlawed by legal consensus; yet it was widely agreed that the enemy leaders had committed acts that were morally, if not legally, outrageous. Many of the leaders were convicted and executed. Most people act as though they believe legal, moral, or ethical restraints are relevant to international behavior.

The Pacifist Position

A very different position from the realist's "anything goes" (in a good cause?) is that of the pacifist. A completely pacifist position may result from a philosophical and moral predilection for nonviolence, a rejection in principle of force as an instrument of national policy, a belief in the spiritually regenerative effect of a nonviolent response to violence, or an overriding concern for the preservation of human life.

Pacifism has deep roots in a number of secular and religious traditions. It seems to have been the dominant view in the early Christian church before the Roman Emperor Constantine converted to Christianity. The Roman Empire was pagan and often persecuted Christians; no Christian could rightly serve in the army of such a power. Pacifism is not the dominant tradition in more recent or contemporary Christianity, but it is still a moderately common and respected view in many Christian churches. It is a basic principle of the Society of Friends (the Quakers) and was practiced by Martin Luther King in his program of civil disobedience against racial segregation. Mohandas Gandhi blended part of this Christian pacifist tradition with deep roots in Hinduism in his resistance to British colonialism, and his example has had great influence on subsequent nonviolent political movements worldwide.

A position that may be pacifist in the context of nuclear war emerges from applying the principle of proportionality: that, by some calculus, the potential gains from an act must be proportional to the harm that may be inflicted. Very many observers conclude that, in any modern thermonuclear war, the costs would inevitably outweigh the gains. Many people who want to avoid both war and submission to aggression have discussed and practiced plans for nonviolent resistance—war without weapons against a would-be conqueror.[2]

Norms for the Resort to and Conduct of War

Between the two ends of the spectrum are a variety of positions. Real interests and values are at stake in international relations.

For those who accept the use of force as a legitimate instrument of state policy in many but not all circumstances, there are two principal moral foci for viewing its limitations. The first concentrates on what conditions justify an initial resort to physical violence and is typically less concerned with the manner in which the conflict is conducted once begun. The second focus adds some norms to govern the conduct of war.[3]

In the American philosophical tradition, often the only just war is one undertaken in self-defense. Self-defense by this definition includes (1) defense of one's allies in keeping with a formal commitment; (2) assistance to a small power under the principle of collective security when authorized by an international organization, such as the United Nations, even if there is no treaty commitment; and (3) assistance to another government in response to its request for aid. Furthermore, the self to be defended is generally defined broadly to include not merely the physical territory but also the values and way of life believed to characterize the nation. No grievances, however severe, would by this definition justify the initiation of war; grievances should always be subject only to negotiation or arbitration or ultimately lived with in the hope they will become more tolerable through the evolution of circumstances. (This position can become a politically very conservative one and is rejected by those who declare that oppression and exploitation must be resisted by force if necessary. Furthermore, once a war in self-defense is undertaken, limits on both the political objectives to be achieved and the means to be used in pursuit of them become very hard to establish.)

The most common Marxist view holds that a war need not be undertaken in self-defense to be justifiable but may be perfectly right if its purpose is to redress class oppression or national subjugation. In this respect it differs widely from the classical American doctrine. Even for the Marxist, however, the war, to be just, must not have a reactionary effect. Specifically, a nuclear war that would result in the annihilation of capitalist *and* socialist civilizations would not be initiated; not just any hypothetical war undertaken by a Communist or Third World country would be permissible.

LIMITING WAR

A quite different position, some version of which is still typical of mainstream thinkers in both the Protestant and Catholic churches, stems from the tradition of Christian moralists, developed after the early days of the church.[4] The position begins from a recognition that all attempts to limit only the *resort* to war are subject to abuse, and it seeks to supplement them with rules for the *conduct* of war. Relevant elements of this tradition regarding the conditions under which a war may be "just" include the following points:

1. The war must be declared by a legitimate authority. (Mere banditry and terrorism are forbidden.)
2. Those who resort to war must have a right intention; this means substantially that they must do so in self-defense or to correct a legitimate grievance (the definition of which varies).
3. The injury the war is intended to prevent must be real and certain. (Obviously, the latter term is elastic.)
4. War must be undertaken only as a last resort.
5. There must be reasonable hope of success; that is, hopeless resistance cannot be justified.
6. The measures employed in the war must themselves be moral (for example, the fair treatment of prisoners and respect for the inviolability of noncombatants).
7. The seriousness of the injury to be prevented must be proportional to the damages that are inflicted.

A further principle, that of double effect, is frequently applied to the evaluation of particular courses of action during the war; that is, the evil done (for example, killing innocent civilians) by any act must not be willed, but only tolerated. This criterion obviously is subject to abuse, but it does still offer the potential for important restraints. By precisely this principle, it would be permissible to bomb missile sites near cities, even though some civilians would be killed by the bombing (thus violating point 6, the principle of discrimination), provided that the other conditions were met (especially point 7, the principle of propor-

tionality). But saturation bombing, deliberate aerial bombardment of predominantly civilian targets, and using larger bombs than strictly necessary to destroy the military target would be condemned. (So, too, would the atomic bombing of Hiroshima and Nagasaki have been condemned. While the purpose may have been laudable—to end the war and save lives, Japanese as well as American—it would not have been considered permissible deliberately to kill those Japanese civilians in order to save others—in effect using the civilians targeted as the means to others' preservation.)

Certainly, these criteria for just conduct in war are not capable of precise measurement by the objective observer. Some deal with interior motives; others concern estimates of the probability of various outcomes, about which there may always be disagreement. But their purpose is less to provide a basis for judgment on others' acts than to offer some standards for internalized restraint. That kind of restraint might be more effective than merely trying to judge wars by their causes and ends, when it is so easy to consider oneself wronged. Although the principles can be used as arguments to justify almost any act, they derive from a tradition that intended them to be strict restraints—most wars could not easily satisfy the conditions.

While the criteria as listed stem most clearly from the Christian tradition, they have earlier origins in ancient Greek and Roman thought, and they provide a basis for very similar positions among non-Christian thinkers. Other contributions to the "just war tradition" include the chivalric code of the Middle Ages, when the knightly profession protected noncombatants, and the development of international law, beginning with Hugo Grotius in the seventeenth century. In this age of cultural diversity and the decline of church authority, it is not enough just to invoke classic writers. Rather, in the words of an author of a recent and important exposition of the tradition, "moral authority . . . has to do with the capacity to evoke commonly accepted principles in persuasive ways and to apply them to particular cases."[5]

The distinction between combatants and noncombatants, so important to the principles just described, is not easy to make

in practice. Modern war requires large armies, mobilization of the entire economy, and the promotion of patriotic fervor among the masses. Many soldiers are draftees, not volunteers; many civilians willingly make munitions or otherwise assist the war effort. Yet while the spectrum is blurred in the middle, a clear distinction is apparent between the soldier and the child, and most of us would acknowledge some obligations to spare the child. The distinction is based in natural justice, that a person who does not make war should not have war made against him or her. A consensus reached in the nineteenth century is expressed in the international law of Article 25 of the Hague Conference of 1907: "The attack or bombardment by whatever means, of towns, villages, dwellings, or buildings which are undefended is prohibited."[6]

Wartime Experience

These limits evolved before the era of aerial bombing and applied chiefly to land warfare. In World War I, the first major conflict fought with aircraft and dirigibles, aerial warfare was conducted against civilians as well as against military targets. That experience, coupled with later bombing (in the Spanish Civil War, by the Italians in Ethiopia, and by the Japanese against Chinese civilians), prepared the governments of Europe for the worst in 1939. But in fact, Hitler avoided making attacks on civilians in France and England for almost the first year of World War II, limiting the Luftwaffe to strictly military targets. He was less restrained in the Blitzkrieg on Poland, but even there, civilian deaths occurred largely as a result of tactical air support of ground forces. Since Hitler was no great humanitarian, his motives were governed by self-interest: He feared the effect that allied bombing of Berlin and other German cities might have on German morale, so he wanted to avoid initiating an exchange of city strikes. Furthermore, he hoped for an early compromise peace. By withholding his air arm, he could avoid antagonizing his enemies unnecessarily and also retain an implicit threat to initiate something worse if they did not cease fighting. Britain and France, for their part, recognized their inferiority in aircraft

and knew that if anyone did start attacking cities, they would suffer more damage themselves than they could return to the Germans.

The limits deteriorated somewhat during the first half of 1940. Rotterdam, Holland, was bombed in May, but that still was not the city of a major belligerent with its own retaliatory capacity. The Royal Air Force began to hit industrial targets in the Ruhr, and during the battle of Britain in August, German bombers attacked aircraft plants as well as air bases. Some civilians were killed by misses or the result of bad navigation. (In early night bombing by the British, 50 percent of the bombs fell beyond three miles of their aim point!) Yet the capital cities of London and Berlin were spared, and there was absolutely no terror bombing deliberately directed against British or German populated areas. Then, on August 24, a few German planes, off course due to a navigational error, dropped some bombs within the city limits of London. Prime Minister Churchill chose to interpret this as a deliberate attack, for which he ordered retaliation against civilian areas of Berlin. Hitler responded with his own escalation, and with the blitz initiated a rapid and ultimately near-complete breakdown of targeting restraints on both sides.

During the rest of the war, saturation terror attacks became routine. On the Axis side, they included the V-1 and V-2 bombs late in the war. As for the Allies, the British habitually attacked at night, when precision bombing was impossible, deliberately directing many of their strikes against residential areas to undermine popular morale. The Americans, too, as in their attack on the open and militarily insignificant city of Dresden, occasionally deliberately went after cities. In the American firebomb raids on Japanese cities, a ring of fire was carefully built to trap people inside. In the March 9, 1945, firebomb attack on Tokyo, 84,000 people died; in Dresden, 135,000 died. These precedents had eroded nearly all moral restraints by the time President Truman had to make the decision about bombing Hiroshima.

The point is not that most of World War II was fought with little restraint on bombing civilian areas—that is obvious; rather, it is important that for quite some time each side did limit its actions and was aware that the other side was doing the same.

Neither moral nor self-interest restraints were entirely put aside at the outset. The former were in sufficiently many people's minds that President Roosevelt characterized the earliest, mildest German air attacks on Poland as "inhuman barbarism which has profoundly shocked the conscience of humanity."

The observed limits, for whatever reasons, should be remembered as well as the unrestricted bombing of the later years. In his announcement of the first atomic bombing, Truman declared, "Sixteen hours ago an American airplane dropped one bomb on Hiroshima, an important Japanese army base." In reality, the presence of the army base was incidental—Hiroshima was chosen for its effect in the killing of civilians. But as a matter of public relations, it still seemed necessary to maintain some appearance of military necessity.

Countercity or City Avoidance?

Since World War II, the conflict betwen two strategies—deliberately targeting population centers and trying to avoid them—has continued. For a while it looked as though a policy of deterring by attacking (or at least threatening to attack) cities was firmly established. On the basis of their own precedent in Japan, American military planners simply assumed that in future years nuclear weapons would be used against cities to detroy the enemy's economy, society, and morale. In addition, the threat of such usage was to constitute the primary deterrent to war. In the 1948–1949 controversy over the B-36 bomber, a number of United States Navy officers argued that countercity war was immoral, but their objections were largely dismissed as rationalizations to further their service's interests. The basic countercity strategy remained essentially unquestioned until the late 1950s in the United States and in other countries as well. Since World War II every major power, either in that conflict or in colonial wars thereafter (for example, the French in Algeria and against Tunisia), made deliberate air attacks on civilians. With nuclear deterrence, deliberately holding civilians hostage became official policy for the first time since the Middle Ages.

By the end of the 1950s, however, second thoughts began to emerge. The problem of how to defend Western Europe became more perplexing in ways that have recently been further intensified. NATO's conventional (nonnuclear) strength has rarely seemed fully adequate to deter a full-scale Soviet conventional attack or to defend Western Europe effectively once war began. American military officers and diplomats have continually tried to persuade the Europeans to spend more for conventional defense, but the results have always been meager. No European state can, by itself, adequately provide for its own defense by conventional means. The Soviet and East European potential invading forces are just too powerful. Europeans have preferred, therefore, to depend primarily on the military forces of their NATO allies (principally the United States) and to make little effort above and beyond what was necessary to meet a minimum level of American demands (and so keep the United States committed to Europe's defense).

The nature of the international relationship (small powers who even with great effort could not do much for themselves, the presence of a big-power ally who does have the resources to make a difference, and the absence of any coercive instrument or taxation that can require common effort by the allies) makes this imbalance of effort almost unavoidable.[7] It is further magnified by the fact that for Europeans a full-scale defense even with modern conventional weapons—multiplying the damage experienced in World War II—might hardly be distinguishable from the effects of nuclear war. Hence they typically have preferred to rely on the American nuclear deterrent for protection and have avoided developing the capability for (and thus the temptation to use) large-scale conventional forces.

One possible way out of the conflict of interest, some Americans thought, would be to use tactical nuclear weapons for the defense of Western Europe. Tactical nuclear weapons could be supplied in large numbers relatively cheaply by the United States. These weapons could then rectify the Western weakness caused by the imbalance of conventional forces. Henry Kissinger first gained fame by his advocacy of this strategy, and it became government policy, so the United States now has more than

6000 nuclear warheads based in Europe. The official rationale has always been that tactical nuclear weapons (some smaller and some larger than the bombs dropped on Hiroshima and Nagasaki) could be used without too great damage to civilian lives and structures and that a war might be halted—by negotiation—before it escalated into full-scale strikes against civilian targets. The enhanced radiation (neutron) bomb represents the latest incarnation of this strategy—a weapon that supposedly could be used against soldiers in the field but that, because of its relatively low blast effects, would cause less damage to nearby civilian structures than would a regular nuclear explosion.

Most observers regard the assumptions underlying the idea of tactical or limited nuclear war in Europe as, at best, questionable. Such an idea often assumes (as did the initial decision to deploy nuclear weapons in Europe) that the West has a quantitative or qualitative advantage in such weapons, an advantage that is as likely to be eroded as was the original western nuclear superiority. It assumes that harrassed battlefield commanders can, with fragmentary information, reliably discriminate between military and civilian targets, know whether the enemy is also maintaining the distinction, and strictly control their own use. It assumes that the Russians cooperate and do not deliberately drive their forces through or very near the cities. It also assumes that, in a densely populated area like Europe, the whole distinction really is meaningful. (Ironically indicating his disbelief in that assumption, an American military commander remarked, "European towns are only a couple of kilotons apart.") For all these reasons the nuclear defense of Europe in Europe has little appeal for Europeans, and the prospects of limited nuclear war in that theatre are not promising. In the words of a former deputy commander-in-chief of the U.S. Army in Europe, "From my experience in combat, there is no way that (nuclear escalation) . . . can be controlled because of the lack of information, the pressure of time, and the deadly results that are taking place on both sides of the battle line."[8]

Efforts to develop a doctrine and capability for limiting nuclear war face a somewhat different set of constraints on the strategic level, that is, on the level of direct Soviet–American

confrontation involving targets in the superpowers' homelands. The idea of limited central war began to emerge a bit later than did that of tactical nuclear war and was expressed officially by then–Secretary of Defense Robert McNamara in his famous Ann Arbor statement of 1962: "Principal military objectives, in the event of a nuclear war stemming from a major attack on the Alliance, should be the destruction of the enemy's military forces, not of his civilian population." Thus massive retaliation was to give way to city avoidance, controlled response, and the hope of reciprocation from the enemy.

In fact, the United States has always had some capability to distinguish between civilian and military targets. McNamara tried to strengthen that distinction in doctrine, improve the ability to maintain it under wartime conditions, and obtain Soviet cooperation. In most respects, the effort failed, and his own 1968 posture statement to Congress explicitly keyed deterrence to an ability to destroy the enemy's major population and industrial centers. A full city-avoidance strategy could have been interpreted as equivalent to counterforce in the sense of striking, instead, against enemy strategic nuclear forces. By that interpretation, a counterforce doctrine could be highly destabilizing in a crisis. Moreover, there was little sign that Soviet officials had any desire to reciprocate by adopting a similar policy. On the contrary, the Soviet Union has given almost no overt encouragement to hopes for any extended avoidance of counterpopulation war once nuclear weapons were used at all. Soviet President Brezhnev, for example, declared in August, 1980, "Statements about alleged limited and partial use of nuclear weapons have nothing in common with reality."

Nonetheless, efforts to elaborate and reinforce a distinction between civilian and military targets have not ceased. During the Vietnam War, McNamara himself, along with other American policy makers, maintained the distinction in practice to a significant degree. In bombing North Vietnam, population centers *per se* were never hit, and some otherwise eligible military targets were spared for fear of too-heavy civilian casualties. River dikes, whose breaching would have flooded the lands of millions of people, were never touched. Near the end of the war

these distinctions tended to break down, chiefly with the "carpet bombing" rationalized by Kissinger "to cause pain" and affect the peace negotiations. And in the counterinsurgency war in South Vietnam, of course, the civilian–military distinction was so blurred that villages and other civilian groupings were regularly attacked.

Countercombatant Targeting

A doctrine and capability for controlled response recognize the very real possibility that the first nuclear weapon fired will not be the consequence of pushing an American button. The first shot may come from some Soviet commander, from a smaller nuclear power, or even from a terrorist. Under those conditions, it would be necessary for the American President to be able to make a limited action in return, not reflexively to initiate an all-out strike on the Soviet Union. There always remains the possibility that nuclear war may occur despite our best efforts to avoid it. Should that happen, it would be disastrous if there were no prior plans to try to avoid population targets. In the words of former Defense Secretary Harold Brown:

> My own view remains that a full-scale thermonuclear exchange would constitute an unprecedented disaster for the Soviet Union and for the United States. And I am not at all persuaded that what started as a demonstration, or even a tightly controlled use of the strategic forces for larger purposes, could be kept from escalating to a full-scale thermonuclear exchange. But all of us have to recognize, equally, that there are large uncertainties on this score, and that it should be in everyone's interest to minimize the probability of the most destructive escalation and halt the exchange before it reached catastrophic proportions. . . . In our planning, we take full account of the fact that the things that are highly valued by the Soviet leadership include not only the lives and prosperity of the peoples of the Soviet Union, but the military, industrial and political sources of power of the regime itself. . . . The notion that, somehow, our only available response to enemy attacks on allied targets would be to strike at enemy cities is incorrect.[9]

Talk of war fighting and first strike threatens to lead to a new round of the arms race as each side tries to find new weapons to deny such a capability to the other—a capability that probably is no longer really attainable as long as both sides do strive vigorously to counter it. Even more seriously, it threatens to erode the stability of mutual deterrence in crisis. A first-strike capability for either side would pose a fundamental danger to deterrence and war avoidance. Any proposal for a shift in nuclear strategy must be subjected to the following three tests:

1. If the proposal were implemented, would it offer prospects that war would be less destructive, or at least not more destructive, than if it were not implemented?
2. Does the proposal offer prospects that war would be less likely, or at least not more likely, than if it were not implemented?
3. Is the proposal consistent with arms-race stability; that is, does it imply less, or at least not additional, armament expenditure?

In logic, the proposal must obtain an affirmative answer to the strong form of at least one of the preceding questions; that is, it must offer a prospect of less damaging or less likely war or fewer expenditures. If it also produces an affirmative answer to at least the weak forms of the remaining two questions (no increment in war damage or war likelihood and no increment in spending), then the proposal will be dominant over the status quo; presumably, it should be implemented unless a better proposal comes along. But if it produces an unfavorable answer to one or two of the questions, then some hard tradeoffs have to be made: Would a diminution in the expected damage from war compensate for some increase in the likelihood of war, or vice versa? Or how much additional spending are we willing to undertake for the prospect of diminishing the expected damage or probability of war?

One version of an alternative strategy has been termed a "countercombatant" strategy, directed to military targets with the aim of sharply reducing the number of expected civilian casualties. The proposal is directed at the first question above.

It does not offer much chance of affirmative answers to the strong forms of the second and third questions, and the answers to the second and third may well be negative, for reasons we shall discuss.

A strategy of countercombatant targeting must preserve the confidence of Soviet leaders that they have an invulnerable second-strike force capable of surviving any American first strike. But it could be consistent with strategic stability if it depended for its effectiveness primarily not on a threat to enemy nuclear retaliatory capabilities but to the enemy's ability to maintain internal security and to control its borders and neighbors by tactical means. Thus, special targets would be arms factories and concentrations of troops and materials for tactical military forces (headquarters, supply centers, marshaling yards and repair facilities, transportation centers, pipelines and fuel-distribution centers, and power plants), particularly those isolated enough to be destroyed with minimum residual damage to the civilian population. Particular attention would be given to Soviet divisions in Eastern Europe and along the Chinese border and to KGB (Soviet internal police) units, often of substantial size, intended for deployment against civilian unrest. Troops of China and of the Soviets' East European allies would be carefully spared. The purpose of all of this is not to destroy the entire Red Army—that would be impossible and in any case quite unnecessary; rather, it is to destroy the Soviet government's ability to use troops. After a substantial number of the kinds of targets listed had been destroyed, the Soviet government would lack assurance that it could repress civil dissent, control its East European allies, or maintain its borders in Eastern Europe, especially with China.

This strategy, then, would be directed against targets deliberately chosen for their political significance and tailored to the particular domestic and international conditions of the Soviet Union. Domestic dissent, especially in urban metropolitan centers such as Moscow and Leningrad, is a problem for the leadership, even if we do not credit the notion that the government is wildly unpopular. More serious is the continued existence of separatist sentiment in many of the republics, such as the Ukraine,

Byelorussia, Georgia, and the former Baltic states. A crippling of the lines of political authority would certainly revive such aspirations. The popularity of Soviet control in Eastern Europe also remains limited, and virtually every one of the USSR's European neighbors has a long-standing boundary dispute with it. Irredentist sentiment in Finland, Poland, East Germany, Czechoslovakia, and Rumania would surely seek to exploit opportunities, and the profound Soviet fear of China hardly needs emphasis.

Would a nuclear war fought under this strategy actually pose prospects of being less destructive than one fought under a predominantly countercity strategy? Certainly, no one could imagine that no civilians would be killed by targeting Soviet war-fighting capabilities, even if the target set were not enlarged to include industry and infrastructure necessary for economic recovery. Many civilians, probably millions, would be in the targets or so near them that they would die in the initial strikes. The Office of Technology Assessment, for example, estimates that an attack only on Soviet oil production capacity, using 79 warheads, would kill between 800,000 and 1.5 million people immediately in collateral damage. A United States attack on the Soviet ICBM force, depending on some technical assumptions and conditions, would kill between 1 percent and 10 percent of the Soviet population as prompt fatalities, and millions more would die from radioactive fallout and the civil distruption that would follow any large-scale nuclear strike.[10]

These examples are merely illustrative and not necessarily the targets that would be chosen (a strike against Soviet ICBMs, for instance, sounds like a first-strike capability). Nuclear war would not lose its horror-provoking capacity, nor would such a strike necessarily look very limited to those on the receiving end. Hence the chances of keeping the subsequent response limited must be evaluated very skeptically. Still, responsible decision makers should make the attempt to limit civilian casualties rather than seek to increase them. This can be done, in some degree, if nuclear weapons are chosen and employed to minimize fallout and if they are of a size no greater than is necessary to destroy their military targets.

A policy of abstaining from deliberate strikes against cities could apply even after a Soviet attack that hit some American urban centers. At that point, an American strike against Soviet population centers as such could serve no purpose other than vengeance—vengeance against a people in no way responsible for the reckless acts by their government.

The difficulties of implementing such a strategy—the requirements for very tight command, control, and communication—are nevertheless very formidable, as we shall see. It is doubtful whether any attempt to have a controlled response could succeed under the conditions of fear, stress, and time pressures of war. The prospects for success would be nil if, as some analysts suggest, the Soviet central leadership and command-and-control facilities are deliberately targeted. Such a strategy seemed implied in many of the discussions of Presidential Directive 59 (PD-59, issued in 1980) on the grounds that making the Soviet leaders themselves the certain targets would constitute the strongest deterrent. Perhaps—but if the Soviet leadership or its command structure were successfully hit, what would then limit and control the Soviet response, or how could the war possibly be terminated by negotiation?

Countercombatant or limited-response strategies may make sense as attempts to control the violence of a nuclear war once it has been begun by the other side. The prospects for success in nuclear-war limitation are, nevertheless, very low. No sane decision maker should imagine they are high enough to make the risks of starting a nuclear war worthwhile. Limited response may make sense only as a desperate policy coupled with a determination never to use nuclear weapons first.

Would such a strategy at least not increase the likelihood of nuclear war? A positive answer depends on the assumption that a threat to the political control of political leaders of any country is as good a deterrent as is a threat to the survival of the populace. It also requires that the country making the threat does not create (or imagine it has) a force that would permit it to conduct a first strike.

Would such a strategy avoid a new round in the arms race? The answer would be "yes" only if those employing the strategy

were confident that existing or cheaply obtainable forces could indeed provide an adequate deterrent and the opponents were confident that a first-strike strategy was neither feasible nor contemplated against them.

EXTENDED DETERRENCE

It is precisely this question of first-strike capability that is at issue in much of the current debate. This debate stems from policies initiated in the Nixon administration that carry the special imprint of James Schlesinger, then Secretary of Defense. Although some flexibility had long been incorporated in the design of the U.S. targeting priorities (the Single Integrated Operational Plan, or SIOP), there was not enough actual preparation to implement it; for example, during the five years of his presidency, Lyndon Johnson was reported to have had just one 20-minute briefing on the SIOP. Schlesinger felt it necessary to strengthen flexibility at all levels of the targeting process. The efforts he began were continued, at least verbally, under the Carter and Reagan administrations. The strongest policy statement in this vein was in PD-59. Its rationale was stated rather clearly by the Secretary of Defense in the Carter administration, Harold Brown:

> But deterrence must restrain a far wider range of threats than just massive attacks on U.S. cities. We seek to deter any adversary from any course of action that could lead to general nuclear war. Our strategic forces also must deter nuclear attacks on smaller sets of targets in the U.S. military forces, and be a wall against nuclear coercion of, or an attack on, our friends and allies. And strategic forces, in conjunction with theater nuclear forces, must contribute to deterrence of conventional aggression as well.[11]

These considerations have been further exemplified by remarks made in 1981 by President Reagan and former Secretary of State Haig about the possibility of fighting a limited nuclear war or firing a "demonstration shot" in Europe.

Extended deterrence remains the crucial problem—how to deter an attack on an area the United States government considers vital to its interests. Areas where conventional attacks might occur include Western Europe, certainly, and perhaps South Korea and the Persian Gulf. Should Israel someday be at risk of being overrun in a conventional war, it (or, conceivably, the United States) might want to raise the nuclear threat explicitly. Wherever and whenever the United States and its allies are in a position of marked conventional inferiority vis-à-vis the Soviet Union and its allies, this remains a problem. Reliance on nuclear weapons represents an attempt to raise the threatened level of violence and so to deter an attack when the ability or willingness to resist such an attack by only conventional means is lacking. Yet, the American nuclear predominance of Cuban missile crisis times is, as we noted in earlier chapters, irreparably vanished. The United States could not make a full-scale strike against Soviet cities without inevitably suffering comparable damage in return. Thus no rational American decision maker will deliberately order such a first strike. Limited options and controlled response are efforts to avoid this dilemma. It is imagined that they might offer a chance to warn the Soviet Union very concretely about the risks it was running of damage to itself and further escalation, including the very real risks that the response could not be controlled for very long. *Perhaps* the Russians would then halt, withdraw, or negotiate.

One attitude often expressed is that the United States must have the ability to avoid losing a war at any level of nuclear escalation. If the United States had such an ability, and if one could assume that the process of escalation could be fully controlled by rational actors (perhaps a heroic assumption), then indeed the Soviet Union would never have an incentive to escalate a conflict. Acquiring and controlling such a capability, however, is far more difficult than theorizing about it. One macabre description of the current posture is: "If there is a conventional war in Europe, we lose. Then we escalate to limited nuclear war, and we lose. Then we blow up the world."

In the words of one article, "war at any level can be *won or lost.*"[12] Or, in the terms of a 1982 directive from Secretary of

Defense Weinberger to the military services, "Should deterrence fail and strategic nuclear war with the USSR occur, the United States must prevail and be able to force the Soviet Union to seek earliest termination of hostilities on terms favorable to the United States." Such goals lead to acquisition of such weapons as the MX for possible first-strike purposes and to large-scale civil-defense programs to evacuate or shelter the American urban population on the assumption that casualties could be kept to some tolerable level: "Domestic damage limitation is not an optional extra—it is a vital necessity if the SIOP is to have any operational value."[13] Of course, meaningful damage limitation simply may not be available for the United States!

The idea of not losing a war implies that the United States should emerge from the holocaust not markedly worse off than the Soviet Union. The level of damage on both sides might be awesome, but the Soviets should have no margin of superiority in the rubble that they might be able to exploit in the postwar world. That position, rather gruesome though it is, rested at the heart of mutual-assured-destruction strategies and the efforts epitomized by terms like *essential equivalance*.

The "war winners" are saying something much more radical. They imply that the United States could carry out strikes, and limit damage to itself, in a way that would leave the United States with a meaningful political and military edge over the Soviets. Their argument imagines that the United States could have the physical capability to wield such damage and the ability to limit damage to itself by civil defense or active defense (ABMs). It assumes that the American people would actually be willing to devote the truly enormous resources it would require even to make a serious try. It implies that the Soviets will lack the ability, or the will, to match American efforts. It implies that the American top leadership is tougher (more willing to risk great damage to itself and its people) than is the Soviet leadership. It implies actually fighting a nuclear war—one that could last for days or weeks—of precise blow, counterblow, and damage assessment. It is an obscene joke.

C³I

Most people who have thought about arms control over the past decades are profoundly disturbed by the talk about war fighting, war winning, and first strike. They are especially disturbed by the assumption that limiting nuclear war is really possible or even probable enough to tempt anyone to begin it. The critical assumption is that command, control, communication, and intelligence (C³I) is, or can be made, adequate to give any confidence that a nuclear war could be kept limited. When one moves from the world of Pentagon or think-tank war games to the real world, some of the difficulties underlying that assumption become more apparent.

A rational Soviet decision maker, if he had really decided to attack the United States or had determined that an American attack on him was probable, would make American C³I facilities his primary target. C³I facilities—not the land-based ICBMs, on which so much public attention has fastened—are the most valuable and vulnerable targets in nuclear war. "Even 50 nuclear weapons are probably sufficient to eliminate the ability to direct U.S. strategic forces to coherent purposes."[14] Many of these C³I facilities are in or near major cities. They depend on telephone switching centers of the civilian Bell Telephone System, again located in major cities. Would an attack on them be distinguishable from a countercity attack? Strategic Air Command (SAC) headquarters is not seriously hardened. North American Air Defense (NORAD) headquarters is hardened, being 1200 to 1400 feet under Cheyenne Mountain. But a 20 megaton warhead with current accuracy would have a 95-percent probability of destroying even a target hardened to 5000 pounds per square inch— far more than NORAD.[15] No hardened shelters for military or civilian leaders exist in Washington, D.C. Soviet Yankee-class missile submarines off the Atlantic coast could hit Washington with less than 10 minutes' warning. Could the President receive word and make and implement a decision in that amount of time? Who would be both constitutionally empowered *and* physically able to take command once the President no longer existed?

The principal facility for controlling the United States nuclear force is the World Wide Military Command and Control System (WWMCCS, or "Wimex"). It operates virtually all significant military communications, not just those relevant to nuclear war. Under wartime conditions, it would be greatly overloaded. Even in peacetime it has been beset with human and operational difficulties; it has never worked properly even in relatively low-level crises, such as those involving the *Pueblo* (with North Korea), the *Mayaguez* (with Cambodia) or the *Liberty* (with Israel). Its complex computer technology is unreliable and beyond the understanding of those who must use it.[16] How, then, could it be relied upon in a nuclear attack, in which case it would be placed under conditions of gross information overload in some respects and extreme system degradation in others (due to physical destruction)?

Systems not physically damaged are likely to be subject to electromagnetic pulses (EMP) that could disable equipment from your stereo set to most military communications. A few suitably placed one-megaton nuclear explosions (perhaps only one, 200 miles over Omaha, Nebraska) could have that effect throughout the continental United States, with peak fields of 50,000 volts per meter.

Communications and observations satellites are already becoming vulnerable to conventional (non-nuclear) attack. The submarine missile-launching force, the most survivable component of the triad, is in fact the component least suited for a strategy of controlled escalation as communication with those submarines is especially vulnerable. One attempted solution was an extremely low frequency (ELF) transmission site in Wisconsin or Michigan with 6000 miles of antennas. Political, economic, ecological, and technological objections forced it to be scaled down to the current plan for "Austere ELF" with only a 130-mile antenna system. There were doubts about the efficacy of the original system; would the scaled-down system suffice? At best, its extremely low frequency means that it would take minutes to send even the shortest message. ELF is not expected to survive a direct attack.[17]

The hot line for communication between the superpowers' top leadership works by satellite. It is at least redundant (in that both Soviet and American systems are available), but the sending and receiving stations are on the ground in Washington and Moscow. "Once the use of as many as 10 or more nuclear weapons directly against the USSR is seriously contemplated, U.S. strategic commanders will likely insist on attacking the full array of Soviet military targets. Political motives for engaging in limited strategic attacks will not likely prevail against the risks of leaving a vulnerable command system exposed to counterattack from a severely provoked enemy.... If national commanders seriously attempted to implement this strategy [controlled response] in a war with existing and currently projected U.S. forces, the result would not be a finely controlled strategic campaign. The more likely result would be the collapse of U.S. forces into isolated units undertaking retaliation on their own initiative against a wide variety of targets at unpredictable moments...."[18]

The notion of limited nuclear war requires not just good but absolutely reliable C³I capabilities. The Reagan administration has committed $18 billion to improving the strategic command structure over the next five years. "Complete implementation of all those programs optimistically might allow the command system to survive moderate levels of attack (50–150 weapons) and to exercise coordinating functions for a few hours to a few weeks."[19] Is that good enough? Even if it were, are Soviet electronics as good as ours? The Pershing II missiles to be deployed in Western Europe will be able to hit targets in Moscow, with high accuracy, after only about 5 minutes' flight time. How can anyone confidently imagine even terminating, let alone fighting, a limited nulcear war under such conditions?

The deliberate initiation of limited nuclear war would be an act of folly, staking the future of civilization in the Northern Hemisphere on the throw of dice loaded against it. Contemplating it marks the bankruptcy of policy. The thought arises from the problem of extended deterrence—how to meet American commitments and protect truly vital American interests in places like Europe and the Middle East. We cannot repeatedly threaten mutual destruction in return for any violation of na-

tional interest. Deterrence may have only a small chance of failing in any particular confrontation or in any year. But over years and decades of crises and continued reliance on nuclear deterrence, the repeated risks are just too high.

Rejection of the notion of limited nuclear war cannot be divorced from considering the problem of how else to defend American allies and interests. One solution, of course, would be isolationism—a determination that there are no such vital interests and that our allies should be left to fend for themselves. That solution seems unlikely. While America could perhaps survive, the costs in security, living standards, and, ultimately, political freedom would be too high for most citizens to tolerate. The problem must be addressed, not wished away.

DEFENDING EUROPE

One attempted solution has been, as we noted earlier, the plan for limited tactical nuclear war in Europe. The idea is that a nuclear war confined to Europe might be kept limited, at least for a time, even if strategic nuclear war involving the American and Soviet heartlands could not. This, too, is a mirage. It is even doubtful that with current weapons, doctrine, and planning, a conventional war could be kept limited for any appreciable time. A substantial conventional attack would almost surely lead to nuclear war. The United States has more than 6000 nuclear weapons based in Europe; the French, hundreds more. In a condition of high alert, those nuclear weapons would probably be dispersed from their storage "igloos" even before war began. To keep them at their storage centers would leave them too vulnerable to a first strike. Yet their dispersal would likely be accompanied by release of the Permissive Action Link (PAL) codes, which permit the actual use of those weapons. At the point of dispersal and decentralization, control over nuclear weapons would pass to low-level army officers—including those of allied countries, not just Americans. With such authority delegated, controlled escalation and bargaining would become impossible. Neither the President nor SACEUR (the NATO com-

mander, always an American) would in fact be able to prevent use of the weapons. A batallion commander, surrounded and endangered, could use those weapons. The prospect of these events could trigger Soviet preemption.

The problem here represents a fundamental dilemma of nuclear command and control. Control should be tight and centralized in the hands of the very top civilian and military leaders. But too-great centralization runs the risk that, if the top leadership is incapacitated, there can be no nuclear response at all; hence the certainty of response, essential to successful deterrence, is degraded. In this case, the weapons and PAL codes would be released to avoid this latter horn of the dilemma. Some balance must always be struck and the balance is never likely to be very satisfactory.

Regardless of what happens with American nuclear weapons, it is French policy to employ their own tactical nulcear weapons in Germany before enemy forces reach French territory. Europeans are aware of this; their awareness of the near certainty of devastation of their countries in nuclear war is at the heart of the current European disarmament movement. If full-scale war were imminent, some European chiefs of state might well opt out of NATO and declare neutrality.

The uncontrollability of nuclear weapons in Europe perhaps makes a terrific deterrent strategy—it deters, for any rational Soviet leader, *any* military move against Western Europe. It implies that, in the event of war, even if we wished to avoid the use of nuclear weapons to save our own skins, we could not. As long as one thinks all Soviet leaders are fully rational—and always fully in control of their own military forces and of political events—that may be a good strategy. But if one believes that events are not always controllable or that significant conventional conflict might arise in Europe inadvertently, it does not look so good. One could, for instance, fear that East–West conflict might arise from some nearly autonomous chain of acts— such as a revolt in East Germany, help to their East German brethren extended by West German citizens and some military units, Soviet military involvement, conflict spilling across the border, and so on. Such a chain of events is improbable but not

quite fanciful. War—and nuclear war—could arise without anyone willing it.

NO FIRST USE

Nuclear war would likely be an act of national suicide rather than an act of rational policy. Therefore, if vital interests outside the United States borders must be defended, it is imperative to seek other ways to defend them. We live in a world where military force is still contemplated and where very large military forces exist ready for use. The defense of vital interests therefore must be undertaken predominately by conventional military forces, not by nuclear weapons. Readiness to use conventional forces in extreme necessity should be coupled with a doctrine of preparation, of physical capability, and of public declaration that the United States will not be the first to use nuclear weapons. In June, 1982, Secretary Brezhnev made precisely this pledge. It would be in the interest of the United States to do so even if the Soviet Union had not.

This is not a prescription guaranteed to be popular. It could be expensive. While it would require the elimination or much more secure storage of some nuclear weapons, it would require new expenditures for conventional forces. Nevertheless, these costs should not be exaggerated. Part of the solution lies in changing force structures, tactics, and types of weapons (for example, more antitank missiles than tanks) rather than just buying more weapons. Nor is NATO inferiority in Europe severe even now. Warsaw Pact divisions are more numerous than are those of NATO, but they are smaller. In actual ground-manpower on the central front, the Pact has an advantage of only 1.2 million troops to 1.09 million for NATO. Of the 58 Warsaw Pact divisions, 15 are Polish and 10 are Czechoslovakian—of doubtful reliability. (Perhaps they should be subtracted from the Soviet total rather than added to it.) In time, Soviet forces from within Russia could reinforce those in the central front, but there are limits to this, both in readiness and in the need to keep large forces on the Chinese border. NATO forces would also bring in

reserves, and troops from America would be met with preplaced supplies and equipment in Europe.

The conventional defense of Europe is very far from hopeless. While not advocating a no-first-use posture, the Supreme Allied Commander in Europe does support stronger conventional forces so as to raise the threshhold of conflict before nuclear weapons had to be used. He reports a NATO study that adequate conventional defense could be achieved by a 4 percent real increase in NATO military spending over six years.[20] In the words of four former national security advisers, "Even if careful analysis did show that the necessary conventional posture would require greater funding, it would be the best bargain ever offered."[21]

Other objections to a no-first-use policy require attention. We might again need a draft to provide enough manpower. The governments of some of our allies would not be happy with it; it would require them to make substantial expenditures and sacrifices that they had been able to avoid while sheltered under the American nuclear umbrella. Europeans do not want to fight a conventional war in Europe either, for good reason. It would raise some temptation for them to create their own nuclear forces, with serious implications for nuclear proliferation. It is not a policy to be embraced lightly or with enthusiasm. But neither is the continued acceptance of policies that seriously contemplate limiting the unlimitable—nuclear war.

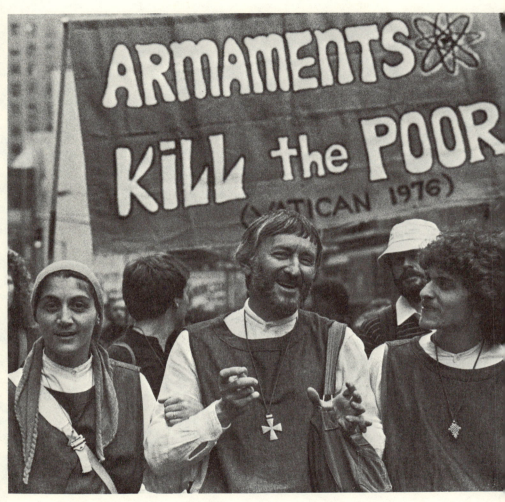

Disarmament rally, New York City, June 12, 1982. (*National Catholic Reporter/ Mary Rieser.*)

8

Arms Control in Perspective

History is not events, but people. And it is not just people remembering, it is people acting and living their past in the present.

Jacob Bronowski, *The Ascent of Man*

Early Arms-Control Efforts

The history of arms-control and disarmament efforts is checkered. Some have succeeded splendidly; others were merely paper agreements with the expectation of little real effect; still others were unambiguous failures.

The oldest arms-control agreement still in effect, and without doubt one of the most successful, is the Rush–Bagot Agreement signed between the United States and Great Britain on April 29, 1817. In it, both sides agreed to limit their naval forces on the Great Lakes to a few small revenue cutters. It was actually a disarmament agreement and not just arms control: Some of the naval vessels then on the lakes had been built there and were too big to be sailed out through the then-existing waterway; they had to be dismantled. The agreement formed the basis for the condition of 3000 miles of unfortified border that citizens of the United States and Canada now take for granted.

We have a stable condition of peace between the two countries, with neither party having even a remote fear of military action by the other or an intention of initiating any military act itself. Given this mutual confidence, it seems natural that the border should be undefended. In 1817, however, it must have seemed anything but natural. The United States and Britain (then the ruler of Canada) had concluded a major war only two years earlier. During that war, they fought several naval battles on the Great Lakes. Substantial portions of the border were still in dispute and were the subject of some acrimony. Peace could not be assumed. Nevertheless, the two states concluded an agreement in the hope that peace would ensue, and the agreement, by reducing tensions, in fact contributed to fulfillment of that hope.

The Washington Naval Conference of 1921, culminating in a treaty the following year, is the most dramatic example of negotiated disarmament in the twentieth century. The conference was intended to consider limitations on naval armaments and fortifications. In opening it, the American Secretary of State, Charles Evans Hughes, astonished the delegates by proposing a sweeping plan for halting new construction, scrapping existing ships, and establishing a parity of naval strength, at reduced levels, among the biggest naval powers. The consequent agreement called for a ratio in capital ships of 5 each for the United States and Britain, 3 for Japan, and 1.7 each for France and Italy. It covered battleships and aircraft carriers and was extended, by the London Naval Treaty of 1930, to include cruisers. No new capital ships were to be built for 10 years, and the strict limitations on tonnage required the powers to scrap 68 ships. For some signatories most of the ships scrapped were old, but for the United States they included 15 new ships costing $300 million.

America, which had embarked on an expansion program that would have made it by far the world's preeminent naval power, made the greatest material concession. Britain had for centuries depended on the Royal Navy to protect herself and her empire and until World War I had insisted on maintaining a navy equal in strength to that of the two next-biggest fleets combined. After the war that was clearly beyond her resources, but many Brit-

ishers wanted at least to maintain superiority over the single next-greatest fleet—America's. The war, however, had so weakened Britain's economy that even that effort would have required enormous sacrifice. The acceptance of parity with America and assured superiority over anyone else came with some sense of relief, if not enthusiasm. The Japanese, with ambitions to great power status and fears for their security, very reluctantly accepted an inferior position at 60 percent of the American and British quotas. Japan too, however, lacked the resources to compete in an all-out race with the United States, and in accepting fewer ships extracted an important concession from Britain and America: that they would not strengthen or add any fortifications in the Pacific between Hawaii and Singapore. Japanese resentment nevertheless simmered, and militarists used the agreement to discredit the liberal government that accepted it. A more nationalist Japanese regime abrogated the agreement in 1934 and then proceeded with rapid naval expansion.

The treaty was acceptable, in 1921, because of extreme war-weariness among the great powers and tight economic conditions. The exertions of a shipbuilding race promised to be very strenuous. Perhaps, by avoiding an arms race in the 1920s, the treaty helped produce the prosperity (least evident in Britain) of that decade. Had all the major economies been equally flourishing in 1921, limitation would have seemed less necessary. The treaty represented a dramatic cut in armaments, not merely a cap on existing forces or the beginning of a slow step-by-step process of reduction. Its initial success was probably due largely to its audacity. Nor was it followed readily or effectively by further naval or military reductions. It took another 8 years to work out an agreement to limit cruiser strengths, and that pact lasted a mere 4 years. The treaty postponed a big naval race for a decade and a half and possibly helped avoid a war during that period (though it is hard to imagine a war in that period, anyway). But it may have contributed to the rise of extremist political forces in Japan and prevented the British and, especially, the Americans from widening their military and naval advantage over the Japanese. In the early days of World War II, the Allies paid dearly for their weakness, which might have

been averted without the treaty; on the other hand, a vigorous naval race might well have exacerbated political tensions between them and Japan, thus leading to World War II by a slightly different route than was actually taken. In political terms it represents neither a clear success nor a clear failure for the concepts of arms control and disarmament.

The years since World War II have seen few acts of real disarmament and still fewer negotiated acts. The SALT negotiations, for example, limited and controlled arms but required almost no destruction or dismantling of existing arms. It is important to keep in mind a distinction: *Arms control is not necessarily disarmament.* Arms control is a process that produces agreements on weapons and the use of weapons—types, how and where they are deployed, their characteristics, safety conditions to prevent accidents, and so forth; arms-control agreements often are concerned with the creation of stability in the sense that neither side is tempted (as in T of prisoners' dilemma) to use the weapons first. The aim of *disarmament* is to reduce the numbers of weapons. Thus, arms control may be seen as a distraction from the quest for disarmament. Alternatively, some kinds of disarmament could work against stability (such as by reducing second-strike capabilities). These possible contradictions produce serious conflicts within the ranks of those who wish to reduce the threat of war.

A list of acts that did approximate some kind of disarmament since 1945 would include the Soviet Union's withdrawal of its missiles and nuclear-capable bombers from Cuba and the dismantlement of their launching facilities after the Cuban missile crisis in 1962. But that was imposed upon them by the United States, with its strategic and local superiority, and was not matched by comparable American disarmament. Other negotiated agreements—but calling for disarmament by one one side in turn for political concessions from the other—include Israeli withdrawal from the Sinai after the Camp David agreements. The Austrian State Treaty of 1955 resulted in American, British, and Soviet withdrawal from the occupation zones in Austria based on agreements guaranteeing the neutrality of an independent and united Austria. This, however, concerned only a

small country and did not prove to be a precedent for reunification of Germany. (If a reunited Germany should violate the neutrality accord and tip to either side, the impact would be immensely greater than that of little Austria.)

The United States can accurately be described as having unilaterally disarmed after World War II, when millions of soldiers and sailors were discharged and immense quantities of equipment scrapped or put into mothballs. It was thought both unnecessary and prohibitively burdensome to maintain such large forces in peacetime. Other powers, including Britain and—to a lesser extent—the Soviet Union, did the same, but none of the force reductions was negotiated or was even the subject of consultation. On a much smaller scale, American military forces were similarly reduced after the Vietnam War, partly because the national political mood demanded a reduction of military effort and partly out of hope (largely dashed) that the Soviets would similarly show restraint. Probably the greatest single act of disarmament over the past 35 years came as a consequence of the Iranian Revolution of 1979. Many officers and technicians were discharged or killed, equipment was allowed to deteriorate, and $8 billion worth of arms purchases from abroad were cancelled. It was unilateral disarmament at a single stroke, but not necessarily a model for international agreement: The disarmament, coupled with vigorous political hostility toward Iran's neighbors, only invited an attack by Iraq.

Any general conclusion to be drawn from these experiences must be that substantial disarmament by two or more states can happen, but only rarely. Under most circumstances, the power of entrenched economic, political, and bureaucratic interests is so strong that they can resist disarmament efforts easily. Only under exceptional conditions, such as widespread revulsion against a recent and especially burdensome war, can the inertia of established patterns of armament be sharply broken. This is not to say that it is pointless to propose or study disarmament initiatives—historic junctures when real disarmament can occur do arise, often with little warning. When they do, it is good to have well-thought-out plans and ideas—intellectual capital, so to speak—ready for use. But expectations of substantial disar-

mament in the context of recent Soviet–American relations, even during the period of détente, would seem misplaced. Hopes for limiting the arms race and avoiding nuclear Armageddon probably are better placed on some form of arms control.

Arms-Control Efforts After World War II

Table 8-1 lists the major arms-control agreements that have been reached since 1959. The final column indicates whether they were bilateral (United States–Soviet) agreements or wider, multilateral agreements. A quick review of them will indicate their principal goals and methods.

Most of the United States–Soviet bilateral agreements have been directed toward the avoidance of nuclear war between the superpowers. The "Hot Line" Agreements of 1963 and 1971, the Nuclear Accidents Agreement of 1971, the High Seas Agreement of 1972, and the Nuclear War Prevention Agreement of 1973 are all devoted principally to providing both sides with information—particularly information on intentions and particularly in time of accident or crisis, when such information is most crucial. The SALT II agreement of 1979 also provided for some means of verification to assure each side that the agreements on limitations of types and numbers of weapons were being kept.

The 1972 and 1974 ABM agreements sharply limited each side's acquisition of antiballistic missile systems. An effective ABM system might have provided substantial protection for population centers—a very difficult feat. While that may sound benign, it contradicts the principal of mutual assured destruction, whereby each side's own population becomes hostage to that side's responsible behavior. A successful ABM system could have destabilized the balance of terror by reducing one side's confidence in its ability to retaliate. (The 1974 agreement called for dismantling one ABM site—but each party had already decided that that system would not be useful anyway.) The SALT I and SALT II Offensive Arms agreements also were intended to contribute to strategic stability by limiting the types and num-

bers of weapons that could be deployed. This would, in at least some small degree, slow the possible destabilizing effects of technological change and also in some degree limit the wasteful effects of arms-race spending.

The multilateral treaties principally have different aims from those of the bilateral agreements. Their goals—still largely arms control—have been to prevent the spread of weapons of mass destruction to types of weapons, places, and countries where they had not already been deployed. Thus, the Antarctic, Outer Space, Sea Bed, and Environmental Modification treaties all provided that the signatories would continue not to do something they had not yet done. The Biological Weapons Convention called for destroying some stocks of weapons, but most analysts of modern warfare techniques agree that both biological and chemical weapons are generally inferior to nuclear weapons as a means of killing large numbers of people; that is, if a state already has large stocks of nuclear weapons, then chemical and—especially—biological weapons are largely superfluous except for small encounters. Thus, the most important targets of the Biological Weapons Convention were the nonnuclear states.

The focusing of multilateral arms-control agreements on the nonnuclear states is, of course, clearest in the Treaty of Tlatelolco (for a Latin American nuclear free zone) and, particularly, in the Nonproliferation Treaty (NPT). Most countries have signed and ratified the NPT, but 32 have not. Many of the nonsignatories are important: France and Spain; China, Vietnam, and North Korea; Algeria; Israel and Saudi Arabia; India and Pakistan; South Africa; and Cuba, Argentina, Brazil, and Chile. States that do not already have nuclear weapons but are parties to the treaty promise not to acquire them, and states that do have nuclear weapons agree not to transfer them to presently nonnuclear states. Surely this is directed toward reducing the risk of nuclear war, both war between currently nonnuclear states and catalytic war (a war initially involving third parties that spreads to draw in a superpower). The acquisition of nuclear weapons by Middle Eastern states is especially feared because of the substantial likelihood that any nuclear war between Arabs and Israelis would spill over into a Soviet–American confrontation.

Table 8-1
Major Arms Control Agreements

Date Signed	Agreement	Provisions	Multilateral (M) or Bilateral USA–USSR (B)
1959	Antarctic Treaty	Prohibits all military activity in Antarctic area.	M
1963	Partial Nuclear Test Ban Treaty	Prohibits nuclear explosions in the atmosphere, in outer space, and under water.	M
1963	"Hot Line" Agreement	Establishes direct radio and telegraph communications between United States and USSR for use in emergency.	B
1967	Outer Space Treaty	Prohibits all military activity in outer space, including the moon and other celestial bodies.	M
1967	Treaty of Tlatelolco	Prohibits nuclear weapons in Latin America.	M
1968	Nonproliferation Treaty	Prohibits acquisition of nuclear weapons by nonnuclear nations.	M
1971	Sea Bed Treaty	Prohibits emplacement of nuclear weapons and other weapons of mass destruction on ocean floor or subsoil thereof.	M
1971	"Hot Line" Modernization Agreement	Increases reliability of original "hot line" system by adding two satellite-communications circuits.	B
1971	Nuclear Accidents Agreement	Institutes various measures to reduce risk of accidental nuclear war between the United States and the USSR.	B

Year	Agreement	Description	
1972	High Seas Agreement	Provides for measures to help prevent dangerous incidents on or over the high seas involving ships and aircraft of both parties.	B
1972	SALT I ABM Treaty	Limits deployment of antiballistic-missile systems to two sites in each country. Reduced to one site by 1974 agreement.	B
1972	SALT I Interim Offensive Arms Agreement	Provides for five-year freeze on aggregate number of fixed land-based intercontinental ballistic missiles (ICBMs) and submarine-launched ballistic missiles (SLBMs) on each side. Later extended to 1980.	B
1972	Biological Weapons Convention	Prohibits development, production and stockpiling of bacteriological and toxin weapons and requires destruction of existing biological weapons.	M
1973	Nuclear War Prevention Agreement	Institutes various measures to help avert outbreak of nuclear war in crisis situations.	B
1974	Threshold Nuclear Test Band Treaty	Prohibits underground tests of nuclear weapons with explosive yields greater than 150 kilotons. NOT RATIFIED.	B
1976	Peaceful Nuclear Explosions Treaty	Bars explosions greater than 150 kilotons for "peaceful purposes" such as excavation or mining. NOT RATIFIED.	B
1977	Environmental Modification Convention	Prohibits military or other hostile use of environmental modification techniques.	M
1979	SALT II Offensive Arms Agreement	Limits numbers and types of strategic nuclear delivery vehicles. NOT RATIFIED.	B

Nonproliferation agreements also help to maintain the over-whelming superiority of the two superpowers over everyone else. Even among the superpowers, this superiority is evident. In 1982, the United States had over 9000 deliverable strategic warheads; the Soviet Union, about 8000. The equivalent number for the third-ranking country, Britain, was not greater than 240. Nonproliferation agreements, *if effective*, ensure that there will be no other challengers to superpower nuclear bipolarity.

Leaders of nonnuclear countries, even when they see the dangers of nuclear proliferation and support limitations, also often resent the superpowers' nuclear dominance. Many have demanded that continued enforcement of nonproliferation agreements depend on the superpowers' willingness not just to pursue arms control but also to accept some measure of nuclear disarmament. They refer to the superpower arms race as "vertical proliferation"; this was a principal focus of the United Nations Special Session on Disarmament, held in 1978 at the insistence of "neutralist" and other Third World countries and despite a distinct lack of enthusiasm from the superpowers. The message of Alva Myrdal's book *The Game of Disarmament: How the United States and Russia Run the Arms Race* is contained in its title. Myrdal charges: "Behind their outwardly often fierce disagreements...there has always been a secret and undeclared collusion between the superpowers. Neither of them has wanted to be restrained by effective disarmament measures." For her, the reason is rooted in international politics: "Military competition results in an ever-increasing superiority—militarily and technologically—of the already overstrong superpowers, thus sharpening the discrimination against all lesser powers."[1] To her, the game is "duopoly" with the superpowers; they do not merely stimulate each other to acquire ever-more expensive and sophisticated weapons but, in so doing, also continually outpace any military force available to any other state or combination of states by an enormous margin.

To support her argument, Myrdal notes the failure of the SALT agreements to produce any disarmament by the superpowers or even effectively to limit the acquisition of qualitatively more horrendous weapons systems. The NPT commits the superpow-

ers to negotiate a reduction in their nuclear arsenals; they have not in fact done so. Says Myrdal, "Only when the arms race has reached a point where some type of bomb or delivery vehicle is obsolete or further weapons development has lost any military usefulness to the superpowers will a gesture of 'disarmament' be made."[2] The superpowers retain, as key elements of both doctrine and preparation, the option of first use of nuclear weapons in response to even conventional attacks by each other or by each other's allies anywhere in the world.

Whether or not her argument is basically correct, much of the world professes to agree with it. K. Subrahmanyam, former director of the Institute for Defense Studies and Analyses in New Delhi, India, wrote that the price of the superpowers' strategy "is to convert the nuclear issue into a confrontation between North and South, and make the development of nuclear technology a symbol of declaration of autonomy from neo-colonialist dependence."[3]

The Proliferation Problem

The proliferation problem has two distinct dimensions. One is the acquisition of material and know-how for governments to make bombs. New nuclear powers will lack the experience of current nuclear powers in controlling the use of such weapons and will lack resources for the elaborate command-and-control capabilities required (this is especially true of the less developed countries). Also, many of these governments are involved in serious local conflicts, which would increase pressures to use such weapons in warfare.

The second dimension is the opportunity for terrorists to gain control of nuclear material (which may have been acquired by governments for peaceful purposes) or finished weapons. Such terrorists may be based within the countries in question or may, while based far away, simply respond to targets of opportunity for acquiring nuclear materials from governments who are unable to take sufficient security precautions.

In meeting the threat of proliferation by governments, several different kinds of incentives for proliferation must be recognized: Different incentives are important for different countries. For some, the problem of security vis-à-vis present nuclear powers may be paramount (for example, the case of Taiwan regarding China or of Pakistan regarding India). More often, security is sought (for example, by Israel and South Korea) against local powers that are not yet nuclear. Sophisticated conventional weapons are becoming ever more expensive; a minimal nuclear deterrent (about 10 bombs) is quite cheap. For still other states, military security is not a primary concern; rather, they may wish to obtain the prestige of a big power or the technological information that can come from the development of peaceful and military nuclear capabilities (as in the case of Brazil). And for still others (for example, Iran under the Shah), perhaps all three kinds of incentives are involved.

While some further proliferation is inevitable, there is nothing inevitable—in speed, extent, or form—about the process. Two decades from now, we could see less than 1000—or several thousand—nuclear power reactors in countries not now possessing nuclear weapons—reactors with little international control or with reasonably effective international control over their use. We could see 8 or 9 or 30 governments with nuclear weapons in their arsenals. Because there are so many facets to the problem, control must proceed along several fronts.

The Promises and Failures of Arms Control

Very many people—scholars, other citizens, and governmental leaders—have devoted their energies to reducing the prospects of war and the level of arms with which wars might be fought. Nevertheless, our review of arms-control and disarmament efforts during recent decades leaves us with a mixed and not altogether reassuring picture. By some standards, there has been progress: The world at least has not blown up; no nuclear weapon has been exploded in anger since 1945. By historical standards for major-war avoidance, that's a long time. Despite common fears, by 1982 the number of states with nuclear weapons had

not exceeded seven. (Acknowledged nuclear-weapons-owning states were the United States, USSR, Britain, France, and China. India had exploded "a peaceful nuclear device," and Israel was generally believed to have had untested nuclear weapons for years.) There have been international agreements to bar nuclear weapons from any environments (Antarctica, outer space, the sea bed) as well as to prohibit atmospheric testing and proliferation (not accepted, however, by all the relevant states). Various Soviet–American agreements have established procedures for consultation and some quite high limits on weapons deployment.

Yet, this progress is extremely limited when compared with the dangers that nuclear weapons pose to humanity. Proliferation of nuclear weapons now appears much more likely during the next few years. Military spending is increasing again in the United States, and Soviet military spending increased throughout most of the period when American spending declined. If anything, the dangers of an upward spiral in the arms race seem greater now than at any time since détente began after the Cuban missile crises. Superpower crises no doubt will occur again, perhaps over control of parts of the Middle East. In any major crisis, there remains the real possibility of central nuclear war, with the consequent destruction of most life and civilization in the Northern Hemisphere.

Many observers of the SALT process regard it as having reached a dead end, epitomized by the failure to ratify the SALT II Offensive Arms Agreement or the test ban agreements. The Offensive Arms Agreement was widely unpopular, attacked from the left as insufficient (no real disarmament) as well as from the right as perpetuating American inferiority in certain weapons. The treaty went unratified as much from lack of real enthusiasm by many of its supporters as from vigorous opposition. The results were faulty because the process itself was, perhaps inevitably, faulty. The focus on quantitative limits produced interminable wrangles over how to measure and balance different weapons—size, number, accuracy, response time, and so on. Since the force structures of the two powers are so different, symmetry in concessions is almost impossible to achieve. The

internal politics of negotiation are as difficult as the international politics. In order to obtain the grudging support of important internal groups, an administration may have to agree to procure some weapons as dangerous or undesirable as those it wishes to limit by treaty (for example, the Carter administration's decision to buy the MX in a largely vain effort to appease conservative opponents of SALT). Research and development of some weapons may proceed on the rationale that they can be used as bargaining chips to be traded, in negotiations, for concessions by the other side. But once the bureaucratic and technological momentum is well under way, the bargaining chip may acquire a rationale and supporters who are unwilling to give it up. (An example of this is the great difficulty encountered in stopping deployment of ABM in 1972.)

With the disillusionment over the SALT failures, attention is increasingly shifting to carefully focused agreements devoted to especially threatening weapons or situations, to certain kinds of unilateral initiatives that can be beneficial whether or not they are immediately reciprocated, and to arms reductions rather than to ceilings without reductions. Some proposals, such as the freeze with bipartisan support in early 1982, would treat ceilings as only a way station toward substantial reductions. A comprehensive freeze would—at least until the reductions—benefit one power in some aspects (for example, the Soviet Union in numbers of missiles) and the other power in others (for example, the United States in numbers of warheads). It would prevent deployment of more long-range theater weapons in Europe, perhaps giving the Soviet Union some advantage but also avoiding the destabilizing effects that American cruise missiles and highly accurate Pershing II missiles might produce. At the present state of the balance between the superpowers, none of these advantages is likely to be critical. Nevertheless, reduction of arms, especially the more dangerous ones, would have to follow.

A Comprehensive Test Ban

One important arms-control agreement that is probably feasible—given the will—is the Comprehensive Test Ban Treaty. The

Partial Nuclear Test Ban Treaty of 1963 prohibits all nuclear explosions in outer space, in the atmosphere, or under water. It does not rule out underground explosions. Signed in the period after the Cuban missile crisis when both Kennedy and Khruschev were trying to improve relations, it has had some value despite its limitations. It stops pollution of the atmosphere with radioactive material—at least by the signatories, who do not include France and China—which had become a major public health concern of 1963. Moreover, the partial test ban has had one very significant military result: It has prevented complete tests of nuclear explosions on the resistance of hardened missile silos to attack and tests that would measure the "fratricide" effect of a nuclear explosion on the impact of a second incoming warhead. As a result, there are technical uncertainties concerning the true hardness of missile silos and the ability of an attacker to fire two or more missiles, in close sequence, against an ICBM that might try to launch under attack. These uncertainties mean that neither side can be entirely sure how successful a first strike against the other's ICBMs might be. As with the uncertainties about missile accuracies, they might mean that a first strike would be less successful than some technical calculations would suggest (that is, hardening might be more successful and fratricide might be important). A prudent decision maker, faced with the question of whether to launch a first strike, would therefore have reason to hold back.

The partial test ban nevertheless permitted continuing testing of warheads alone. New warheads were needed for the abortive ABM effort and, more importantly, for MIRVs. Had there been a total test ban, effective development of MIRV warheads would have been sharply inhibited. Continued testing of existing warheads for reliability is also considered important by some. Should a decade or more pass with no testing permitted, questions would necessarily arise about the efficacy of weapons that had long been held in the inventory. It is now too late to prevent the emergence of MIRV, but it would be desirable, in most respects, to put a brake on new generations of weapons developments by forbidding nuclear testing. In the long run, doubts

about the reliability of weapons, new or old, should add to the hesitancy of a side contemplating a first strike.

Completion of a comprehensive test ban would have other advantages as well. It could provide new momentum for arms-control negotiations at a time when the pattern of quantitative limits on weapons procurement (as in SALT) has proven to be of low value. Furthermore, it would assist the now-fragile effort to stem the proliferation of nuclear weapons. It would provide concrete evidence that the superpowers were willing to restrict their own nuclear-development efforts and so enhance their credibility in urging others to accept restrictions. A ban on the further production of fissionable material would also help stem proliferation.

The first attempt to conclude a comprehensive ban on nuclear tests foundered over Soviet–American differences about on-site inspection, with the Americans insisting on more than the maximum the Soviet Union was willing to permit (only three). The inability to bridge the inspection gap led instead to the partial test ban, which excluded underground tests because of doubts that such tests could be reliably detected without on-site inspection. Efforts to restrict testing further are reflected in the Threshold Test Ban Treaty of 1973, which placed a limit of 150 kilotons on all underground nuclear explosions, and the Peaceful Nuclear Explosions Treaty of 1976, which barred nuclear explosions greater than 150 kilotons for peaceful purposes, such as mining or excavation. Again, the threshold of 150 kilotons (about 10 times the power of the Hiroshima bomb) was meant to take into account the possibilities of detection by satellite and seismic means without on-site inspection. Neither treaty has been ratified, chiefly because their contribution was thought to be very marginal and to deflect from the more important effort to achieve a comprehensive test ban.

Negotiations for a comprehensive ban proceeded and by 1977 appeared on the edge of success. The Soviet Union offered to permit ten monitoring stations (black boxes) on its territory and to allow on-site inspections in case of questionable occurrences. The Soviets also accepted the American position that ratification of a treaty by China and France (both of whom refused even to

take part in the negotiations) was not necessary. Some minor details still were left for resolution, but basically a comprehensive test ban treaty was ready for signature.

But the treaty remains unsigned. The Carter administration moved it to a back burner in favor of SALT II, and when the public and congressional mood shifted against SALT, the administration feared to go forward with the comprehensive test ban. The Reagan administration has said it is unwilling to conclude a treaty, perhaps from general antipathy to arms-control agreements. Opposition from the weapons laboratories and the Joint Chiefs of Staff (who would prefer to have weapons development unrestricted) is also an important factor with this administration, as is the fact that a comprehensive ban, if signed very quickly, might marginally complicate development of enhanced-radiation weapons (neutron bombs). Yet the Comprehensive Test Ban Treaty remains of great potential benefit and the most readily accessible of any significant arms-control agreement.

Another possibility not yet the subject of serious negotiation and therefore much further from achievement is a ban on testing not warheads but missiles. If the chief threat to land-based missiles stems from the high accuracy of incoming missiles, then a ban on further testing would freeze assurance of accuracy at current levels of knowledge. By the same argument as applied to the uncertainties of warhead functioning, remaining uncertainties about missile accuracy should also give pause to anyone contemplating a first strike. Some uncertainties about missile accuracy will probably be resolved fairly shortly, however—at least excluding those uncertainties that can be removed only by a quite different mode of testing (such as polar trajectories). This ban would thus have to take effect very quickly, and that is unlikely. Also, since the United States still retains an edge in missile accuracy, the Russians probably would not be willing to conclude a test ban that froze their own inferiority.

Outer Space

The 1967 Treaty of Principles Governing the Activities of States in the Exploration and Use of Outer Space prohibited the de-

ployment of all nuclear weapons or other weapons of mass destruction in space and on the moon and other celestial bodies. Other treaties have also regulated the militarization of space. The Partial Test Ban Treaty covered tests in space as well as in the atmosphere. Several have protected national means for verifying that arms-control agreements are being respected, and these national means depend heavily upon satellites. The 1972 ABM Treaty, the 1971 Nuclear Accidents Agreement, and the 1973 Nuclear War Prevention Agreement all require noninterference with satellite warning systems or immediate notification of any interference. The provisions as applied to systems for early warning of attack are especially important; violation would be an extreme provocation and, of course, itself a warning of impending attack.

Major gaps nevertheless remain in the structure of outer space agreements. While nuclear weapons may neither be deployed nor exploded in outer space, there is no provision against testing or deploying nonnuclear means of attacking satellites. Nor is there any provision forbidding testing and deployment of space-based weapons intended against systems other than satellites—for instance, ABMs directed against missiles in the early post-launch phase of their trajectory. Because the technologies of antisatellite and ABM systems are closely linked, it may be impossible to have a verifiable ban on one that does not include the other as well.

The United States spent about $7 billion in 1981 on military space programs; the Soviet Union, a comparable amount. These efforts have sometimes been crucial in warning of missile attack and in providing communications facilities, weather and navigation information, and a variety of military, economic, and intelligence data. Some of the information is valuable in monitoring antagonists' activities; other information, such as mapping, has made possible high accuracies for ICBMs and cruise missiles. It is important to maintain these facilities, which would be threatened by Soviet deployment of significant antisatellite capabilities. If either the United States or the Soviet Union should become able to attack each other's satellites, the elimination or

threatened elimination of early warning would be very destabilizing.

Both sides are, in fact, working on antisatellite systems. The Soviet Union has made repeated tests of its crude interceptors, though through 1981 many of the tests were failures. The United States is developing a small rocket, to be carried under the wing of an F-15 jet fighter, that could ram a satellite at extremely high speed and destroy it. The cost of satellite destroyers promises to be very much cheaper than the satellites themselves, and some people in the American military establishment are anxious to develop them, exploiting our technological lead over the Soviets. This is likely, however, to be a shortsighted view, akin to exploiting the lead the United States once had in developing MIRV; that is, the lead may be only temporary, or, even if the lead is maintained, an inferior Soviet capability may still be quite sufficient to endanger American satellites. If so, the result—mutual vulnerability of systems important to deterrence—would leave both states worse off than before. Competitive antisatellite systems promise the situation of the prisoners' dilemma, and the best result can come from an agreement to avoid the competition in the first place, passing up the temptation for ephemeral gain. Actually, American dependence on space satellites for information is greater than Soviet dependence, owing to our need for high-technology electronics to pierce Soviet secrecy. Failure to reach a mutual agreement to respect satellites might therefore hurt the United States more than the Soviet Union in the long run.

One reason it may be difficult to conclude an agreement to keep weapons out of space is the similarity in technology of some antisatellite systems to possible ABM capabilities. Space-based lasers or possible particle beams could, in principle, be used for either purpose. But both would have very large energy requirements, would demand physical capabilities far greater (even under optimistic assumptions) than currently achievable, and would be extraordinarily expensive (perhaps $100 million per ICBM booster destroyed), costing far more than the boosters themselves.[4] In addition, a practical ABM system would have to work against *many* incoming targets, including decoys.

Given these likely technological demands and costs, it would seem foolhardy to refuse an otherwise desirable ban on outer space weapons for such a long-shot prospect of gain from deployment. The possibility of achieving an effective ABM system may be seductive, but it hardly seems worthwhile to succumb. Even if it were to become feasible, what would happen in the necessarily substantial time between development and full deployment of an operational system? Could we expect the Soviet Union to sit tight until its most reliable deterrent force was nullified? The period immediately preceding effective deployment, rather, would put the Russians into a most uncomfortable use-it-or-lose-it situation. Mutual restraint, if it can be achieved, would be far preferable. But negotiations on this front must proceed rapidly. The further research and development are allowed to go (on both sides), the stronger the forces of technological, bureaucratic, and scientific momentum will be. Opportunities for serious negotiation cannot indefinitely be postponed in the hope of a better international political climate or more reasonable administrations.

The bans on space weapons and nuclear testing are the most obvious and perhaps most readily achievable major negotiable arms-control steps. Neither represents disarmament, but at least they would prevent technological improvements that could threaten the mutual balance of deterrence. While actual disarmament—the dismantling of existing weapons systems—might be more desirable, it would provoke greater resistance. These particular steps are attractive precisely because they offer concrete means of preserving stability.

Independent Initiatives

One attractive kind of disarmament would pinpoint certain particular weapons systems that have become obsolete or are especially undesirable because they threaten the stability of deterrence. It is not enough merely to pick out weapons that are obsolete (for example, to have a bonfire of liquid-fueled ICBMs or first-generation ballistic-missile-launching subs); disposing of weapons that are just obsolete is only an empty public-relations

gesture. The SALT II quantitative limits on delivery-vehicle launchers were criticized on substantially these grounds. The limits were so high that they required very little destruction of existing weapons (disarmament), and where they did require some dismantling, it was clear that the old systems would be the ones to go; that is, the weapons that were of little use anyway would be dismantled. Old Polaris submarines with un-MIRVed missiles would be retired as their useful life expired, but they would be replaced by new Trident subs with the newest, longest-range, most accurate MIRVed missiles.

But some kinds of weapons are both obsolete and undesirable. Arguably, all land-based missiles fall into this category. In Chapter 2, we reviewed the difficulties in finding a secure, invulnerable basing mode for land-based MX missiles. The true situation may well be that there is *no* satisfactory way to make land-based missiles invulnerable. If so, (1) they would be useful, if at all, only for a first strike, not as part of a retaliatory force; (2) they would only make war more likely, and would serve no political purpose to a rational actor; and (3) both the United States and the Soviet Union would benefit from negotiating an agreement to dismantle land-based ICBMs entirely. The permanent absence of this weapons system might benefit both sides, even if other systems (bombers, SLBMs, and perhaps cruise missiles) remained fully in place or were expanded.

The land-based ICBM problem illustrates a further point that must be fully appreciated: Sometimes unilateral arms control or even disarmament acts can be highly advantageous to the power that makes them. Mutual elimination of land-based ICBMs might well be the best outcome, but mutual continued reliance on them may be the worst outcome. If we can get an agreement with the Soviets for mutual ICBM dismantling, we should do so. In May 1982, President Reagan proposed that both sides cut back their land-based ICBMs to 850, with no more than 2500 warheads on such missiles. In principle, the idea seems a good one. Yet, the Soviets' greater reliance on ICBMs (see Figure 8-1; the great majority of their warheads are on land-based missiles, as compared with only a minority of ours) will make them very reluctant to conclude that kind of agreement. Furthermore,

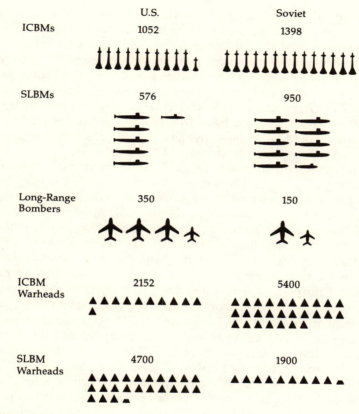

Figure 8-1
Strategic arms, 1982. The numbers are necessarily approximate.

we know that the negotiation of agreements on quantitative reductions is terribly difficult. Rather than continue with essentially no change, a good second-best outcome for the United States might very well be to dismantle its own land-based launchers even without Soviet reciprocation. As potential first-strike forces, perhaps drawing preemptive fire in a crisis, our vulnerable ICBMs threaten us as much as they do the Soviet

Union. Thus, if we cannot persuade the Soviet Union to match our action, it still may be in our interest to get rid of missiles. That would be a unilateral step and disarmament of a sort—but *only* of a sort, since it would imply increased relative, and perhaps absolute, reliance on other kinds of American delivery vehicles. Whereas many varieties of unilateral disarmament would threaten our security, some kinds may actually enhance it.

There is some history of successful unilateral initiatives, or at least of an exchange of concessions by the superpowers without a formal public agreement. In June 1963, President Kennedy, frustrated by the difficulty of negotiating a nuclear test ban treaty, announced that the United States would unilaterally forego further tests. The next month, Khrushchev proposed a limited test ban (which became the basis of the treaty) that would cover all the kinds of tests that could be observed without on-site inspection. In the following year, each side removed about 10,000 troops from the central front in Europe, each reduced its defense budget slightly, and each announced a cut in production of nuclear material for weapons. Some of these concessions were made in secret negotiations; others were unilateral acts small enough not to be damaging to the side that initiated them but perhaps large enough to set a process of reduction into action.

Disarmament

George F. Kennan, in May 1981, gained great attention by urging a 50 percent across-the-board immediate reduction in the two superpowers' nuclear arsenals. Referring to the overkill phenomenon, whereby each power already has more than enough nuclear weapons to destroy the other's society many times over, he correctly identified the current arsenals as excessive for any rational purpose and quite arbitrary in size. No analysis can identify the current levels as ideal for their purpose or necessarily better than the lower levels of ten or twenty years ago. The original decision to build 1000 Minuteman missiles was politically arbitrary—a nice round number—and not based on careful cost–benefit analysis.[5]

Contemporary decisions on how many MIRVS or SLBMs were required are hardly better, especially since how many "we" build inevitably affects how many "they" build, in a spiral completely lacking any obvious equilibrium point. Reductions would save some of the resources now being poured into pointless competitive arms purchases and, by making a dramatic move, perhaps lower international tensions and thus reduce the pressures that might produce war.

Many people despair of arms control—so much has been tried and so little gained. Nuclear deterrence does not seem more stable nor we more secure. If deterrence fails, it seems unimaginable that nuclear weapons could be used in any way that would be morally or ethically defensible. A limited nuclear war is so unlikely; a nuclear exchange could hardly be discriminating or proportional to any achievable political goal. Some religious leaders still pay respect to the principle of deterrence and call for negotiated and mutual disarmament. But their patience wears thin, and they call for "the elimination of nuclear weapons from the earth."[6] Radical disarmament would not end the threat of nuclear weapons, but a drastic cut in nuclear stockpiles could end the threat of the destruction of our Soviet, American, and European societies.

However laudable the aims of major disarmament, it carries its own risks. Problems of verification would be very great, and the negotiations thus would inevitably be drawn out. If too much attention were focused on the problems, other dangerous trends (for example, the race in space or the pressures requiring conclusion of a test ban) might be neglected. It is not clear that either side would even be willing to freeze its relative position at current ratios. We could have very acrimonious debates over whether current Soviet advantages in some aspects of ICBM deployment should be preserved and whether the Soviet Union would tolerate permanent inferiority in sea-based deterrent forces.

There is even a respectable argument that very severe force cuts (actually greater than those proposed by Kennan) would be destabilizing. With 1000 land-based ICBMs, it is hard to imagine a situation requiring extreme accuracy and reliability of incoming missiles, perfect coordination, and so on that would not

leave some significant number (such as 50, or 5 percent) of American ICBMs surviving a first strike. That would still be enough to destroy the major population and industrial centers of the Soviet Union and, under almost any circumstances, to inflict unacceptable damage. But if the number of ICBMs on both sides were cut drastically (say, by 80 percent), the same proportion of surviving missiles (5 percent of 200, or 10) might conceivably not be enough to inflict unacceptable damage under such extreme political conditions as an acute crisis or the impending dissolution of the Soviet empire. At some point, therefore, deterrent stability might actually be reduced. Large-scale conventional disarmament, if it meant a more ready reliance on nuclear deterrence of attacks on allies, could be especially dangerous.

Proposals such as George Kennan's (which, as noted, is not so extreme anyway) must, like all others, be scrutinized carefully for their unanticipated as well as expected effects. Certainly, they do deserve attention and may well be the most promising direction available. In the long term, some reduction in nuclear arsenals surely must occur. We cannot continue with current—or greater—destructive capabilities for the indefinite future without some dire consequence. At the same time, sweeping proposals should not put aside the chance for more restricted but carefully pinpointed specific steps, such as the test ban or space ban. If we are to get to the long term at all, we must meanwhile learn to avoid the most provocative actions and limit the most provocative weapons. Furthermore, arms-control proposals must have appeal in domestic politics. Esoteric measures, such as C^3I improvements, must be carefully explained to the public and made palatable by combining them with some dramatic moves to arms reduction.

Basically, the hope of complete nuclear disarmament must clearly be seen as a fantasy. The knowledge of how to build nuclear weapons cannot be buried. Literally hundreds of thousands of people in the world have the necessary information and skills, and acquisition of fissionable materials is not difficult. We have to worry now about the clandestine procurement of nuclear weapons by relatively small and weak states and about

the acquisition of nuclear explosives by terrorists. How much more would we worry about the secret production of nuclear weapons by a vast, rich, and still-very-closed country like the Soviet Union? If the United States were to make a zero-nuclear-weapons agreement with the Soviet Union, on what level of on-site inspection of Soviet society would we have to insist? Is there *any* degree of inspection that could truly satisfy our anxieties? After all, in a world where no one else had any nuclear weapons, a state that could secretly produce only a few score would be in a commanding position to dictate peace on its own terms. Could we possibly trust the Russians when they had that kind of potential for gain? Nuclear knowledge is very much like the mythical fruit of the Garden—the knowledge cannot be unlearned. We must continue to devise ways to live with the bomb—controlling numbers, reducing incentives to use, restricting access to it wherever possible, finding nonmilitary ways of resolving our conflicts. We remain prisoners of our nuclear knowledge and of the security dilemma of nation-states. We do not know how to wish either out of existence.

Recall Figure 4-1 in Chapter 4, where we discussed the causes of arms races. They are part of a long chain of causation that leads not only to arms races, but ultimately to war. Some of those causes, like population growth, technological advance, and demands for scarce resources, are the same as those that trouble the nightmares of people who worry about limits to growth. By common agreement, the most serious global environmental problems will not emerge until some time in the twenty-first century. But the arms race and war problem is with us now and by many judgments is becoming daily more acute. A new world war would be, thanks to modern technology, overwhelmingly destructive. We thus run the risk that long before the world goes out with an ecological whimper, it may go out with a catastrophic military bang.

Responsibility

Do we live in "that brief interval between the lightning and the thunder"?[7] It is hard for an ordinary citizen—or even a highly educated scientist or other professional—to know how to react. The problems of strategy and war avoidance often seem impossibly complex and intractable. Our readiness to grapple with them is discouraged by the myth that these are all highly technical questions, best left to the experts who have access to esoteric information. Yet, as we noted in the preface, it is largely a false myth, and one that is self-servingly perpetuated by the experts. Nonexperts may never be able to advise which of two competing weapons systems is more cost-efficient. Yet the more important questions—Why should we procure a system like that at all? How will it be perceived by our antagonists and friends? What is the purpose of military force or threat in the world? Do we want the likely outcomes?—are not questions only for the technological expert. They are questions on which we all are competent to express opinions, provided only that we make a conscientious effort to examine information available in the public domain and to clarify the logic of our analyses.

The dangers we face are real. They stem from many causes. Some of those causes we may give moral labels: pride, greed, and malice. Others are a part of the basic human condition not so readily characterized as evil but more nearly as unavoidable: miscalculation, fear, insecurity. In some degree we are locked into a situation by actions, whether correct or wrong, of our predecessors. Most notably, it can do us no good just to wish nuclear weapons had never been invented. The situation is grim and will tax human ingenuity, energy, and good will to the utmost. If there were easy solutions, we would have taken them by now.

But neither is the situation hopeless. We have, after all, come this far without nuclear war. Many people, in 1945, did not expect that much success. The success—such as it is—has not come by accident. It has come because people have puzzled and struggled. Some of those people are scientists, government officials, and military officers. Others are ordinary citizens who,

by their votes and their protests, have forced leaders to take ordinary citizens' fears seriously.

Not only *can* we express such opinions responsibly, but the nature of our political system *requires* us to do so. Democracy in practice frequently falls short of its ideal. Nevertheless, if it is to work at all, its citizens cannot allow the most fundamental issues of life and death to be walled off for expert appraisal only. There is a legal expression that is meant to protect a citizen from the demands of a totalitarian government which requires the citizen's continual overt applause of government policy: *Qui tacit consentire*. According to this principle, a citizen must be presumed to accept a policy in the absence of his or her explicit statement to the contrary. In a democracy, silence about nuclear issues carries an implication not just of indifference but of acceptance. If we stand silent in the face of an arms race—and the war to which it may lead us—we must share responsibility for the outcome. "Silence gives consent."

Notes

CHAPTER 1

1. Paul Doty et al., "Nuclear War by 1999?" *Current*, January 1976: 32–43; and Marguerite Kramer and Bruce Russett, "Images of World Futures," forthcoming.
2. "A Gallup Poll on Nuclear War," *Newsweek*, October 5, 1981: 35; and *Eurobarometer*, 16 (December 1981): 9.
3. Joel S. Witt, "Advances in Antisubmarine Warfare," *Scientific American*, 244, 2 (February 1981): 31–41.
4. Franklin D. Holzman, "Dollars and Rubles: The CIA's Military Estimates," *Bulletin of the Atomic Scientists*, 36, 6 (June 1980): 23–27.

CHAPTER 2

1. Herbert Scoville, *MX: Prescription for Disaster* (Cambridge: MIT Press, 1981).
2. Daniel Graham, *Shall America Be Defended?* (New Rochelle, N.Y.: Arlington House, 1979), pp. 87–88.

3. For a skeptical view of the danger, see John Steinbruner and Thomas Garwin, "Strategic Vulnerability: The Balance Between Prudence and Paranoia," *International Security*, 1, 1 (Summer 1976): 138–181. See also Bernard T. Feld and Kosta Tsipis, "Land-Based Intercontinental Ballistic Missiles," *Scientific American*, 241, 5 (November 1979): 50–61.

4. A. G. B. Metcalf, "Editorial: Missile Accuracy—The Need to Know," *Strategic Review*, 9, 3 (1981): 6.

5. Barry Blechman et al., *Force Without War* (Washington, D.C.: Brookings Institution, 1978), p. 132.

CHAPTER 3

1. Arthur F. Burns, "The Defense Sector and the American Economy," in Seymour Melman, ed., *The War Economy of the United States* (New York: St. Martin's, 1971), p. 115.

2. R. P. Smith, "Military Expenditures and Capitalism," *Cambridge Journal of Economics*, (1977): 61–76; and Dan Smith and R. Smith, *Military Expenditure, Resources and Development* (London: Birbeck College Discussion Paper No. 87, 1980). A good description of the economically distorting effects of the military sector may be found in Jacques Gansler, *The Defense Industry* (Cambridge: MIT Press, 1981).

3. Bruce Russett, *What Price Vigilance? The Burdens of National Defense* (New Haven, Conn.: Yale University Press, 1979), ch. 5.

4. Bruce Russett, "Defense Expenditures and National Well-Being," *American Political Science Review*, 76, 4 (December, 1982).

5. United States Congress, Office of Technology Assessment, *The Effects of Nuclear War* (Washington, D.C.: U.S. Government Printing Office, 1979), pp. 94–95.

6. Arthur M. Katz, *Life After Nuclear War* (Cambridge, Mass.: Ballinger, 1982).

7. U.S. Arms Control and Disarmament Agency and Department of Defense studies, cited in James Fallows, *National Defense* (New York: Random House, 1981), p. 161.

8. Director of Central Intelligence, *Soviet Civil Defense* (Washington, D.C.: Library of Congress, 1978), p. 4.

9. United States Congress, Office of Technology Assessment, op. cit., pp. 100, 105–106.

10. Jonathan Schell, *The Fate of the Earth* (New York: Knopf, 1982).

11. Harrison Brown, *The Human Future Revisited: The World Predicament and Possible Solution* (New York: Norton, 1978), p. 240.

12. Harrison Brown, J. Bonner, and J. Weir, *The Next Hundred Years: Man's Natural and Technological Resources* (New York: Viking, 1954), pp. 21–22.

13. Brown, op. cit., p. 241.

14. Michael D. Wallace, "Armaments and Escalation: Two Competing Hypotheses," *International Studies Quarterly*, 26, 1 (March 1982): 37–56. Some questions can be raised about this analysis and whether the results really are quite so lopsided. Nevertheless, the basic point seems plausible.

15. Bruce Bueno de Mesquita, "Systematic Polarization and the Occurrence and Duration of War," *Journal of Conflict Resolution*, 22, 2 (June 1978): 241–268.

16. Ibid., p. 263. See also Bruce Bueno de Mesquita, "Theories of International Conflict: An Analysis and Appraisal," in Ted Robert Gurr, ed., *Handbook of Political Conflict: Theory and Research* (New York: Free Press, 1980).

17. Alan Ned Sabrosky, "From Bosnia to Sarajevo: A Comparative Discussion of International Crises," *Journal of Conflict Resolution*, 19, 1 (March 1975): 3–24.

18. J. David Singer, "Accounting for International War: The State of the Discipline," *Journal of Peace Research*, 17 (1980). See also A. F. K. Organski and Jacek Kugler, *The War Ledger* (Chicago: University of Chicago Press, 1980), ch. 2; and Charles F. Doran and Wes Parsons, "War and the Cycle of Relative Power," *American Political Science Review*, 74, 4 (December 1980): 947–965.

19. A. F. K. Organski, *World Poltitics*, 2nd ed. (New York: Knopf, 1968), p. 294. Evidence that wars are more common among states nearly equal in power may be found in R. J. Rummel, *The Dimensions of Nations* (Beverly Hills, Calif.: Sage, 1972); and Erich Weede, "Overwhelming Preponderance as a Pacifying Condition Among Asian Dyads," *Journal of Conflict Resolution*, 20, 3 (September 1976): 395–411.

20. Organski, op. cit., p. 480.

21. Ibid., p. 361.

CHAPTER 4

1. Nazli Choucri and Robert C. North, *Nations in Conflict: National Growth and International Violence* (San Francisco: W. H. Freeman and Company, 1975), p. 168.

2. Ibid, p. 169.

3.   *Arms and Insecurity* (Pittsburgh and Chicago: Boxwood and Quadrangle, 1960).

4.   Herbert York, "Multiple Warhead Missiles," *Scientific American*, 28, 2 (1973): 14–25. See also Ted Greenwood, *Making the MIRV* (Cambridge, Mass.: Ballantine, 1975).

5.   Robert J. Art, "Why We Overspend and Underaccomplish: Weapons Procurement and the Military–Industrial Complex," in Steven Rosen, ed., *Testing the Theory of the Military–Industrial Complex* (Lexington, Mass.: D.C. Heath, 1973).

6.   Raymond A. Bauer, Ithiel de Sola Pool, and Anthony Dexter, *American Business and Public Policy: The Politics of Foreign Trade* (New York: Atherton, 1963), p. 142.

7.   Richard M. Nixon, *Six Crises* (New York: Doubleday, 1962).

8.   Miroslav Nincic and Thomas Cusack, "The Political Economy of U.S. Military Spending," *Journal of Peace Research*, 16, 2 (1979): 101–115.

9.   Choucri and North, op. cit., p. 218.

10.   Richard K. Ashley, *The Political Economy of War and Peace* (London: Frances Pinter, 1980).

11.   See Hans Rattinger, "Armaments, Détente, and Bureaucracy," *Journal of Conflict Resolution*, 19, 4 (1975): 571–595; A. F. K. Organski and Jacek Kugler, *The War Ledger* (Chicago; University of Chicago Press, 1980); Jean Christian Lambelet and Urs Luterbacher, "Dynamics of Arms Races: Mutual Stimulation vs. Self-Stimulation," *Journal of Peace Science*, 4, 1 (1979): 49–66; Miroslav Nincic, *The Arms Race* (New York: Praeger, 1982); Steven Majeski and David Jones, "Arms Race Modelling: Causality Analysis and Model Specification," *Journal of Conflict Resolution*, 25, 2 (1981): 259–288; Thomas Cusack and Michael Don Ward, "Military Spending in the United States, Soviet Union, and China," *Journal of Conflict Resolution*, 25, 3 (1981): 429–469; and Michael D. Wallace and J. M. Wilson, "Non-Linear Arms Race Models," *Journal of Peace Research*, 25 (1978): 175–192.

12.   Charles Lucier, "Changes in the Value of Arms Race Parameters," *Journal of Conflict Resolution*, 23, 1 (1979): 17–39.

CHAPTER 5

1.   Anatol Rapoport and Albert Chammah, *Prisoners' Dilemma* (Ann Arbor: University of Michigan Press, 1965); Anatol Rapoport, *Two-Person Game Theory: The Essential Ideas* (Ann Arbor: University of Michigan

Press, 1966); and Steven J. Brams, *Game Theory and Politics* (New York: Free Press, 1975).

2. J. Tedeschi, T. Bonoma, and S. Lindskold, "Threateners' Reactions to Prior Announcement of Behavioral Compliance or Defiance," *Behavioral Science*, 15, 2 (March 1970): 171–180.

3. Charles Osgood, *An Alternative to War or Surrender* (Urbana: University of Illinois Press, 1962).

4. Muzafer Sherif et al., *Intergroup Conflict and Cooperation: The Robbers' Cave Experiment* (Norman: University of Oklahoma Press, 1961).

5. Robert Axelrod, "Effective Choice in the Iterated Prisoners' Dilemma," *Journal of Conflict Resolution*, 24, 1 (March 1980): 3–25.

6. Graham Allison, *Essence of Decision: Explaining the Cuban Missile Crisis* (Boston: Little, Brown, 1971), p. 203.

CHAPTER 6

1. Henry A. Kissinger, *Years of Upheaval* (Boston: Little, Brown, 1982).

2. S. E. Asch, "Effects of Group Pressure upon Modification and Distortion of Judgment," in D. Cartwright and A. Zander, eds., *Group Dynamics, Research and Theory* (Evanston, Ill.: Row, Peterson, 1953), pp. 189–200.

3. Irving Janis, *Victims of Groupthink* (Boston: Houghton Mifflin, 1972), p. 13.

4. David J. Finlay, Ole R. Holsti, and Richard R. Fagen, *Enemies in Politics* (Chicago: Rand-McNally, 1967).

5. William Gamson and Andre Modigliani, *Untangling the Cold War* (Boston: Little, Brown, 1971).

6. George Kennan, *The Cloud of Danger* (Boston: Little, Brown, 1978), pp. 87–88.

7. See Robert Jervis, *Perception and Misperception in International Politics* (Princeton, N.J.: Princeton University Press, 1976); Ole Holsti, *Crisis Escalation War* (Montreal, Quebec: McGill–Queen's University Press, 1972); Michael Brecher, *Decisions in Crisis: Israel, 1967 and 1973* (Berkeley and Los Angeles: University of California Press, 1980); and Irving L. Janis and Leon Mann, *Decision-Making: A Psychological Analysis of Conflict, Choice and Commitment* (New York: Free Press, 1977).

8. See Luc Reyschler, "The Effectiveness of a Pacifist Strategy in Conflict Resolution: An Experimental Study," *Journal of Conflict Resolution*, 23, 2 (June 1979): 228–260; and Stanley Milgram, *Obedience to Authority* (New York: Harper & Row, 1974).

CHAPTER 7

1. See Richard H. Hersh, Diana Pritchard Paolitto, and Joseph Reimer, *Promoting Moral Growth: From Piaget to Kohlberg* (New York: Longman, 1979).

2. Gene Sharp, *The Politics of Nonviolent Action* (Boston: Porter Sargent, 1973); and Anders Boserup and Andrew Mack, *War Without Weapons* (New York: Schocken Books, 1975).

3. Robert W. Tucker, *The Just War* (Baltimore: Johns Hopkins University Press, 1960).

4. See William V. O'Brien, *The Conduct of Just and Limited War* (New York: Praeger, 1981) and Paul Ramsey, *The Just War* (New York: Scribner's, 1968).

5. Michael Walzer, *Just and Unjust Wars* (New York: Basic Books, 1977), p. 288. See also James Turner Johnson, *Just War Tradition and the Restraint of War* (Princeton, N.J.: Princeton University Press, 1981).

6. Carl H. Builder and Morlie H. Graubard, *The International Law of Armed Conflict: Implications for the Concept of Assured Destruction*, (Santa Monica, Calif.: Rand Corporation, 1982, R–2804–FF). These authors argue persuasively that nuclear deterrence as presently practiced is a violation of international law.

7. Bruce Russett, *What Price Vigilance? The Burdens of National Defense* (New Haven, Conn: Yale University Press, 1970), ch. 5.

8. Arthur S. Collins, Jr., "Theatre Nuclear Warfare: The Battlefield," in John F. Reichart and Steven R. Sturm, eds., *American Defense Policy*, 5th ed. (Baltimore: Johns Hopkins University Press, 1982), pp. 359–360.

9. U.S. Department of Defense, *Annual Report, Fiscal Year 1981* (Washington, D.C., January 21, 1980).

10. United States Congress, Office of Technology Assessment, *The Effects of Nuclear War* (Washington, D.C.: U.S. Government Printing Office, 1979).

11. Harold Brown, remarks delivered at the Convocation Ceremonies for the 97th Naval War College Class, Newport, R.I., August 20, 1980.

12. Colin Gray and Keith Payne, "Victory is Possible," *Foreign Policy*, 39 (Summer 1980): 14.

13. Colin Gray, "Presidential Directive 59: Flawed But Useful," *Parameters: Journal of the U.S. Army War College*, 11, 1 (March 1981): 33.

14. John Steinbruner, "Nuclear Decapitation," *Foreign Policy*, 45 (Winter 1981–82): 18.

15. Desmond Ball, "Can Nuclear War Be Controlled?" *Adelphi Paper*, 161, 1981.

16.   William J. Broad, "Computers and the U.S. Military Don't Mix," *Science*, 207, (March 1980): 1183–1187.

17.   Ball, op. cit.

18.   Steinbruner, op. cit., pp. 22–23.

19.   Ibid., p. 25

20.   General Bernard W. Rogers, "The Atlantic Alliance: Prescriptions for a Difficult Decade," *Foreign Affairs*, 60, 5 (Summer 1982): 1145–1156.

21.   McGeorge Bundy, George F. Kennan, Robert McNamara, and Gerard Smith, "Nuclear Weapons and the Atlantic Alliance," *Foreign Affairs*, 60, 4 (Spring 1982): 761.

CHAPTER 8

1.   Alva Myrdal, *The Game of Disarmament: How the United States and Russia Run the Arms Race* (New York: Pantheon, 1976), pp 293–294, 297.

2.   Ibid., p. 222.

3.   K. Subrahmanyam, "The Nuclear Issue and International Security," *Bulletin of the Atomic Scientists*, 33 (Feb. 2, 1977): 20.

4.   Richard L. Garwin, "Are We on the Verge of an Arms Race in Space?" *Bulletin of the Atomic Scientists*, May 1981: 48–53.

5.   Desmond Ball, *Politics and Force Levels* (Berkeley and Los Angeles: University of California Press, 1981).

6.   Resolutions by the American Lutheran Church and the Lutheran Church in America, September 1982.

7.   William Irwin Thompson, *At the Edge of History* (New York: Knopf, 1971), p. 163.

Index

The Prisoners of Insecurity

Contents

3. WHAT'S WRONG WITH ARMS RACES?   47

4. WHY DO ARMS RACES OCCUR?   69

5. CONFLICT AND COOPERATION IN THE ARMS RACE   99

6. DETERRENCE AND CRISIS STABILITY   115

Preface

This book is concerned with how to think about strategic questions. It is not devoted primarily to current information on weapons numbers and capabilities. It has some information of that sort, but its real purpose is to show that most of the fundamental questions about national security and arms control are political rather than technological.

A popular myth says that arms control and security questions should be left to the experts, that these are highly technical, arcane matters about which the ordinary citizen cannot hope to be properly informed. Rather, says the myth, the citizen should leave such matters to those who devote their full professional lives to them and to those who also have access to the highly specialized secret information without which no informed judgment is possible. "If you don't have a high-level security clearance, you have no business dabbling in these affairs."

For the elites who make such an argument, this myth is self-serving. Of course they would prefer to keep effective policy debate within a small "informed" circle. It is a nuisance to have to make policy in a broad democratic forum; such a process is time consuming and has unpredictable outcomes. Yet, arms control is the only area of public policy that is so sharply removed from informed democratic discussion—and it is also probably the most critical area, literally a matter of life and death. To the extent that such a vital area of concern remains removed from informed public debate, democratic government is a sham.

The myth is also very misleading. Of course, some elements of the discussion are highly technical, where intelligent discussion can be carried on only by those who have devoted a lifetime to mastering demanding scientific disciplines. Certainly, there are some questions, such as those about the relative physical capabilities of competing weapons systems, that can be answered only with information that is quite properly kept secret from our international antagonists and from anyone who might leak it to those antagonists. But by far the majority of strategic questions do not demand either highly technical knowledge or secret information.

One important question is, How will this weapon perform? But different experts—with different perspectives and self-interests—will often give different evaluations of the same weapon. Moreover, other questions are fully as important: Why should we acquire this weapon? What political purpose is it supposed to serve? Assuming that the experts are correct about its performance, is that political purpose one we want to encourage? What are the potential costs and benefits to our society—global society as well as national society—from pursuing that purpose? Should we attach great importance to procuring a strategic weapon that has a high probability of surviving an attack against it? Should we seek also to procure a weapon that has a high probability of destroying our opponent's strategic delivery vehicles? What would be the purposes—in pursuit of what national goals—for which such a weapon would be used? Are those the goals we want to pursue? What price—in money, or in greater risk of war—are we prepared to pay in order to pursue those goals? These are not technical questions about "hardware"; they are political questions about our central values. They ask us not to measure the accuracy of a missile but to give a thoughtful, analytical judgment about what kind of country and world we want to live in and what kind of risks we are prepared to assume to get that world.

Other questions are in a sense "technical," but they are not the sort that demands access to highly classified information. Although they do require some specialized data, the data are readily available to anyone who is willing to make a reasonable effort to look for them. For example, What are the prospects of reasonable economic and social recovery after a substantial nuclear war? Information on the degree of physical damage from a nuclear explosion is readily available in numerous public documents. Anyone can do the simple arithmetic necessary to multiply that damage by so many urban targets and can then begin to imagine the total amount of damage that would imply for the nation. Anyone can readily discover where the medical facilities are located that might care for the casualties, whether they would be likely to survive large-scale urban destruction, and the kind of caseload they would have to carry. There is some work involved in garnering such information. It has to be done responsibly, and one may likely find it necessary to consult some experts along the way. But one does not need a top-secret clearance and a Ph.D. from MIT. Sensible discussion is within the reach of an intelligent, diligent citizen who is accustomed to carrying on serious discussion of other public issues.

Clemenceau was right: War *is* too serious a business to be left to the military (or to civilian strategic experts). This book is dedicated to considering some of the basic questions that can and should be asked by the conscientious citizen, questions for which one can and should expect to obtain reasonable (though rarely conclusive) answers. It aims to provide some of the technical information necessary to an informed discussion, a clarification of what the basic political issues really are, and some analytical tools to help achieve clear thinking. It is time to demystify the strategic nuclear debate that will determine the future of our children and grandchildren (and perhaps whether we shall have grandchildren).

Parts of this book were taken from an earlier book co-authored with Harvey Starr, *World Politics: The Menu for Choice* (W. H. Freeman and Company, 1981). Most of the material, however, is new. This book reflects twenty years of professional work on international politics, much of which was devoted to questions of military security and arms control. It is a book by a civilian social scientist, not by a technician, a military officer, or a policy maker. Although each of these other roles certainly qualifies one for some unique contribution to the discussion, I believe the academic social scientist's role also has value for this purpose. I have at one time or another consulted and contracted with government and intergovernmental agencies immediately concerned with matters of security, including the United States Arms Control and Disarmament Agency, the United States State Department, the Advanced Research Projects Agency of the Department of Defense, the Advanced Research Program of the Naval War College, and the Center for Disarmament of the United Nations. To those I should add the RAND Corporation, Bendix Aerospace Division, the United States Catholic Conference, The Pacific Sierra Research Corporation, and the Institute for Defense Analyses in the private sector. I have further benefited from discussions with innumerable government officials, military officers, and fellow academics. I especially want to thank Garry Brewer and Paul Bracken of the School of Organization and Management at Yale University for insights about command and control problems, which I discuss in Chapter 7. Colleagues at other institutions who commented on part or all of the manuscript and to whom I am indebted include Steven Brams, Matthew Bunn, Barry Hughes, Shaul Mischal, George Rathjens, Joseph Romm, Herbert Scoville, Jr., and Kosta Tsipis. Of course, none of these people or organizations bears any responsibility for what now appears between the covers of this book.

September 1982   *Bruce Russett*
                                                New Haven, Connecticut

But we are articled to error . . .
We live in freedom by necessity,
A mountain people dwelling among mountains.

W. H. Auden, *In Time of War*

For
Meg, Mark, Lu, and Dan
that they may be able to choose well

The Prisoners of Insecurity

A Minuteman missile in its underground silo at Ellsworth Air Force Base, South
Dakota. (Courtesy U.S. Air Force.)

1

"Security" Policy and Insecurity

I have examined Man's wonderful inventions. And I tell you that in the arts of life man invents nothing; but in the arts of death he outdoes Nature herself, and produces by chemistry and machinery all the slaughter of plague, pestilence and famine. . . . In the arts of peace, Man is a bungler. . . . His heart is in his weapons.

The Devil, in Act Three of
George Bernard Shaw's *Man and Superman*

MUTUAL VULNERABILITY

Nuclear war is the central terror of our time. Since 1945, humanity has lived in the shadow of the mushroom cloud. At first, the threat took the form of only a few atomic bombs in the hands of one government. Though in awe of their new weapons, most Americans initially thought of the bomb as a means to provide national security and to ensure peace, prosperity, and the American way of life. But other people in other countries looked for military means to secure their own interests. They too armed themselves, and many of them learned how to make nuclear weapons. Now we know that at least five countries have stockpiles of nuclear arms, and other countries could have them very soon. Many of the weapons are now thermonuclear devices, some of them as much as 1000 times bigger than those dropped on the horrified citizens of Hiroshima and Nagasaki. The United States has about 30,000 bombs of all types; the Soviet Union has

1

about the same number. Our search for security has imprisoned us in a cage of insecurity. Americans, Europeans, Russians, and others are all in it together. We are not sure how we got here. And we certainly don't know how to get out.

Much of the time we go about our ordinary lives in ordinary ways. We act as though a nuclear war could not happen or would not devastate us if it did. We put money into our retirement funds. We raise children. But in our hearts we know. Our children know, too. They make anxious jokes about World War III. They dream of mushroom clouds and fireballs. None of us can escape this knowledge.

Our leaders try to reassure us, but they know better, and sometimes they have to say so. President Reagan says, "Everybody would be a loser if there is a nuclear war." Chairman Brezhnev says, "To expect to win a nuclear war is dangerous madness." It would be in the interest of both countries to stop, to negotiate an end to the arms race, to lower the risks of unimaginable catastrophe. Yet they go on. Why?

International politics, like all social life, involves a mixture of conflict and cooperation. In all our relations, even with friends and family, we both compete and cooperate. Usually, in personal affairs, the competitive elements are kept under control because it is so important to maintain the cooperative relationship, at the cost once in a while of giving in to a friend's or relative's interest when it conflicts with ours. With someone we love and with whom we share a sense of identity (husband and wife, parent and child, close friends), it is sometimes a pleasure rather than a sacrifice to give up something for the other. In international politics, however, there is little affection or sense of shared identity. Common interests and the need to maintain a cooperative relationship may seem less immediate; thus we tend much more to emphasize the elements of competition. But we should remember that *both* elements are there and that any effort to achieve our own goals must include some of each.

The truth of this insight is rarely sharper than in the current strategic nuclear arms race between the United States and the Soviet Union. The two superpowers are caught in a "security dilemma" in which the conflicting elements of their relationship often seem to overwhelm the cooperative elements. There is no higher authority, such as a world government, to which they can appeal for protection. Rather, they must try to provide security through policies that heavily emphasize military strength and military deterrence. "Security" resides in the ability to inflict awesome damage on each other in retaliation for any attack, and yet the very ability to inflict retaliatory damage may lead each opponent to fear a deliberate attack. To prevent this, each opponent tries to equip himself with an assured retaliatory capability. Mutual arms strength cannot banish mutual insecurity, but a one-sided failure to arm would produce the insecurity of weakness.

The two superpowers have armed themselves to a position of special insecurity in which both would suffer utter destruction in the event of a big nuclear war. This risk is unprecedented in the history of modern warfare. Nations often fought wars, but the majority of their people could survive: Their societies might be in disarray, but they could be put together again in some form, and the nation itself would likely live. Even World War II, fought to a point of unconditional surrender, brought the collapse of the Nazi and Japanese governments, yet the German and Japanese nations survived.

There can be no assurance of survival after a modern nuclear war. Should such a war happen, hundreds of millions of people would be dead. Industry, agriculture, services, and the government would be shattered. Long-term havoc would be inflicted on the environment from immediate and delayed radioactive fallout. No advanced industrial society that had been subjected to heavy attack would survive in recognizable form. The two great powers would lose together, both absolutely and relative to the Third World and Southern Hemisphere nations not directly in the line of fire. Everybody would suffer from worldwide fallout, depletion of the atmospheric ozone shield, interference with the food chain, and disruption of world trade.

The possibility of nuclear war is not remote, however much we dislike thinking about it. In 1975, a group of experts on strategic questions estimated that the chances of a nuclear war by the year 2000 were about fifty-fifty. In 1977, a group of 400

American and foreign scholars gave their opinions about whether nuclear weapons would be used in a conflict somewhere in the world during the subsequent 25 years. Nearly half thought the odds were greater than even.[1]

Almost four decades have passed since the last major war between great powers. By historical standards, that is a long time. In some respects the passage of time may be comforting. The United States and the Soviet Union have become accustomed to dealing with each other despite their hostility, and they have developed regular means to discuss and negotiate matters that might endanger the peace. Both are sobered by the thought of the bomb and what it could do. But the passage of time may not be fully benign. The once-vivid images of the effects of nuclear weapons on human victims in Hiroshima and Nagasaki have faded.

The very fact that nuclear weapons have not been used since 1945 gives some policy makers a false sense of security that they will not be used or that they might successfully be used in some "limited" or "war-winning" fashion. Ordinary people, however, are becoming very apprehensive about nuclear war and its consequences. In a September 1981 Gallup poll, half of all Americans polled said they believed that any Soviet–American war would lead to all-out nuclear holocaust. In Western Europe over the past decade, the proportion of people who estimated the chances of war within the next 10 years to be greater than fifty-fifty rose from 12 percent to 24 percent.[2] The decline of detente, the failure of the United States to ratify the SALT II Treaty (from the Strategic Arms Limitation Talks), a new round in the strategic arms race, and the increased vulnerability of land-based missiles to surprise attack have all contributed to our fears.

If there should be a large-scale nuclear war, it would be a war without winners in two senses: First, as just indicated, both superpowers would be devastated; second, as we shall see in the next chapter, neither could hope to achieve a significant advantage. It is impossible for either side to launch an attack that could disarm the other—that is, prevent the other from launching a crippling retaliatory blow. Each has more than enough strategic retaliatory forces to survive an attack. Although land-based missiles are becoming vulnerable to attack (there are serious disagreements as to how vulnerable), other types of weapons are much less vulnerable. Long-range bombers are safe if they are in the air. The missiles designed to be launched from submarines (SLBMs) are especially well protected. There is virtually no chance that American missile-launching submarines will become vulnerable even in the 1990s—they are too hard to locate, and Soviet antisubmarine warfare technology lags substantially behind America's.[3] Soviet ICBMs may be somewhat vulnerable individually, but there are so many (about 1400 missiles with a total of more than 5000 warheads in 1982) that American decision makers could have no confidence in their ability to destroy them all. Retaliation would be unavoidable.

Furthermore, the number of weapons on both sides is far greater than the number of targets to be hit. The Soviet Union in 1982 had over 8,000 separately targetable warheads and bombs; the United States had more than 9,000. But the United States has only 2,000 cities with as many as 10,000 people each. Even a "small" Soviet attack on major American population and industrial centers, using just 300 to 400 warheads, would produce 45 million to 70 million casualties and destroy 25 to 35 percent of American industry.

No one anywhere near ground zero, even in shelters, would survive. People might be evacuated from some of the cities if there were days of warning and if they did not panic. They might find fallout shelters in the countryside if many billions of dollars' worth of preparations had been made, or they might even dig them if they had brought their shovels. They could stay in the countryside if the weather were mild and if they had food, water, and medical supplies. Weeks later, when the radiation levels would have dropped, they could come out. They would, as we shall see in Chapter 3, emerge into a wasteland.

The figures above are only for those casualties suffered from immediate blast, heat, and radiation effects during the first 30 days. They say nothing about the other results of an attack: the unknowable—but surely immense—number of casualties from the decimation of physicians and medical facilities; disease and hunger from the rupture of America's interdependent network of transportation, communication, and food- and fuel-shipment facilities; economic and political chaos from the fracture of the country's institutional and financial structure; the still-longer-run effects on food production (grain silos as well as missile silos are concentrated in the Great Plains); and the effects of long-term radiation.

American military and population centers are scattered across the continent; thus a large-scale nuclear war would affect everyone (Figure 1-1). The population of the Soviet Union, despite the country's great physical expanse, is even more concentrated than that of the United States. Two hundred of the Soviet Union's cities contain 62 percent of its industry. The American urban population (131 million people) lives on 18,000 square miles of land; the Soviet urban population (126 million people) occupies only 7,000 square miles. As a result of this concentration, even a few hundred exploding nuclear weapons would wreak horrendous damage.

This picture of far more weapons than available targets gives rise to the expression "overkill." Perhaps many Soviet or American retaliatory weapons could be wiped out in a surprise attack, and there might not be enough retaliatory weapons left to "kill" the same people several times over. But there *would* be enough to kill them once.

The United States has lost forever the security of isolation provided by the oceans and the security of world military dominance it enjoyed in 1945. The arms race—a quest for security through piling up ever-larger numbers of ever-more-sophisticated instruments of destruction—has brought us to an age of insecurity.

THE SOVIET–AMERICAN ARMS RACE

1945–1952: The Period of American Nuclear Monopoly

Both the United States and the Soviet Union disarmed substantially from the high levels of World War II, though the Soviet Union disarmed less than the United States did. During this time, the atomic bomb was the central element in America's

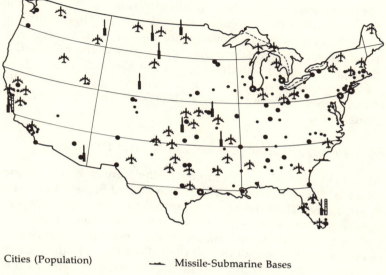

Cities (Population)

· 100,000 to 250,000

● 250,000 to 1,000,000

◉ More than 1,000,000

—— Missile-Submarine Bases

✈ Major Airfields

▮ Missile-Launching Sites

▮▮ Missile-Testing Centers

Figure 1-1
Distribution of potential population targets and military targets in the
United States. [Kevin N. Lewis, "The Prompt and Delayed Effects of
Nuclear War," *Scientific American*, 241, 1 (July 1979):44. Copyright ©
1979 by Scientific American, Inc. All rights reserved.]

posture of deterrence. Although the Soviet Union retained large
land forces—forces that might have threatened Western Europe—the Russians had, for practical purposes, no atomic
weapons. They exploded their first bomb in 1949, but it would
require several more years for the Soviet military to acquire operational weapons. The Americans would have been able to
bomb the Soviet Union and inflict substantial damage, though
the number of American bombs was not large (probably only

about 300 even at the end of this period) and they were fission (atomic), rather than the much more devastating fusion (hydrogen), bombs. With the devastation, disease, famine, and economic dislocation certain to follow any attack, the prospective damage was enough to deter the Soviet Union from any great adventures—especially given that country's great and vividly remembered suffering from World War II and its 20 million casualties.

1953–1957: The Period of American Nuclear Dominance

June 1950 marked the beginning of the Korean War with the attack of Communist North Korea on United States–supported South Korea. The Soviet leaders apparently did not expect any substantial American response to this invasion, but, in fact, the United States intervened militarily in a massive way. Furthermore, as the Americans turned the tide of battle to their favor and penetrated deep into North Korean territory later in the year, the Chinese Communists intervened. The result was a very large land war on the Korean peninsula. Coupled with previous serious incidents in the emerging cold war (the Communist takeover in Czechoslovakia and the Berlin Blockade in 1948; the Communist victory in China and the Russian atomic-bomb explosion in 1949), the Korean War initiated a great American program of rearmament, during which annual U.S. defense expenditures nearly tripled.

The Korean War was a painful experience for the United States in domestic as well as international politics, and American leaders vowed not to fight another such major land war against a Soviet ally. American Secretary of State John Foster Dulles declared in 1954 that the United States would respond to any further Communist attacks on "free world" nations "in a manner and at a place of our own choosing." In other words, the United States would feel free, in the face of any such "proxy war," to strike not at the small Communist ally, but directly at the Soviet Union—a "massive retaliation" with nuclear weapons.

Such a threat was credible because the United States had by then built up a very large stockpile of nuclear weapons and an intercontinental bombing force to deliver them. With the development of the hydrogen bomb (the United States tested the first device in 1952), the amount of damage that could have been inflicted on the Soviet Union was very great indeed and included tens of millions of potential deaths. Although the Russians exploded a multimegaton thermonuclear device in 1953, they lacked both very great numbers of the weapons and adequate means of delivering them to the North American continent. The Americans had the advantage of bases in Europe and Asia that were quite near their opponent, an advantage always denied to the Russians.

The ability to inflict damage was so greatly imbalanced in favor of the United States that we can accurately speak of this as the period of American strategic dominance. In the face of this capacity, the Soviet leaders pursued a very cautious and generally unprovocative foreign policy. Nevertheless, they embarked on a major rearmament effort of their own in response to that of the United States.

Figure 1-2 illustrates the pattern of American and Soviet defense expenditures throughout the post-World War II period in constant (inflation-adjusted) dollars. The heavy solid line represents CIA estimates of what Soviet military spending would be if they had to buy their equipment and pay their soldiers at American prices and wages. The estimates of Soviet military spending are quite rough and are still subject to much controversy. The USSR does not publish accurate military budget data, and various problems arise in creating estimates of total expenditures expressed in dollar terms. In fact, the costs are exaggerated, since, for example, the Soviet conscript army probably costs only about a third as much for pay and upkeep per person as the American volunteer army does. Soviet equipment, though often more numerous than its American counterparts, is generally less sophisticated and of lower quality—valuing a Soviet tank as equivalent in cost to an American tank exaggerates the value of the former. Correcting all these distortions would produce an estimate of Soviet military spending in recent years approximately equal to that of the United States rather than 20 percent higher as suggested by the solid line.[4]

10

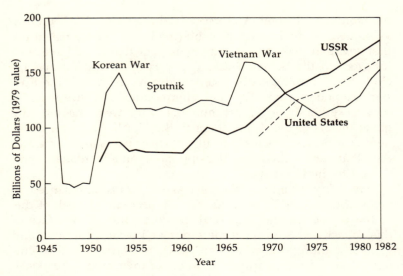

Figure 1-2
Military expenditures of the USSR and the United States, 1945–1982
(billions of 1979 dollars). [Bruce Russett and Bruce Blair, eds., *Progress
in Arms Control? Readings from Scientific American* (San Francisco: W. H.
Freeman, 1979), p. 5, supplemented by material from U.S. Defense
Department, Arms Control and Disarmament Agency; and Stockholm
International Peace Research Institute. Soviet data since 1966 are Amer-
ican CIA estimates. An alternative method (dashed line) of estimating
Soviet expenditures would lower the USSR line by about 10 percent.
See U.S.A.C.D.A., *World Military Expenditures and Arms Transfers, 1968–
1977* (Washington, D.C.: U.S.A.C.D.A., 1979), p. 15.]

Another problem is that a one-to-one comparison of the United
States and the Soviet Union ignores their allies. NATO is bigger
and richer than the Warsaw Pact and spends more on defense.
Using the CIA estimating procedures, NATO as a whole still
outspent the Warsaw Pact by more than 5 percent in 1979 ($206
billion to $195 billion). Even that assumes Soviet "allied" forces
are really an asset to the USSR—but might it not sometimes be
a liability for the Soviets to have well-equipped and not entirely

friendly Polish forces behind them? For all these reasons, the precise spending *levels* of Figure 1-2 should not be taken too seriously, but as a general representation of *trends* and upward or downward *shifts*, the picture is reasonably accurate.

1958–1966: The Period of American Predominance

The degree of American dominance over the Soviet Union decreased during this period, as reflected in the new term to describe American superiority—predominance. Still, it was a time in which the United States could consider the option of a first strike (that is, the initial use of nuclear weapons) on the Soviet Union in response to a proxy war started by a Soviet ally. Despite Soviet rearmament, the Americans retained a very substantial edge in the strategic weapons competition.

Any temptation to relax, however, was eliminated by the shock Americans received in 1957 when the USSR became the first country to put a satellite (*Sputnik*) in orbit around the earth. The Russians could do that only because they had perfected very large rockets—rockets that could be used equally well as intercontinental missiles, the delivery vehicles for nuclear and thermonuclear bombs. The United States was slightly behind in this technology, and there were widespread fears that the Soviet Union would build so many missiles (ICBMs) that they could threaten rapid destruction of American bombers, on which the United States still relied for its deterrent. While this "missile gap" never in fact materialized, the fear of it led to a new crash program of development and deployment of American land- and sea-based intercontinental missiles.

American predominance thus was maintained, although the Soviet Union was increasingly developing an ability to do much wartime damage to the United States (at least in retaliation, even if it could not credibly think about a first strike against the Americans because of expected overwhelming American retaliation). The difference might have been on the order of 5 million to 10 million American deaths and perhaps 50 million Soviet deaths. To remedy this imbalance cheaply, the Soviets in 1962 put a variety of nuclear-armed missiles and bombers into Cuba, less than 100 miles from Florida. Even though the United States still had a very great nuclear edge over the Russians, the American leadership thought this act was serious enough to provoke the Cuban missile crisis. In that 13-day crisis, President Kennedy instituted an air and naval quarantine of Cuba and demanded that the Soviet Union remove all its nuclear-weapons-carrying forces. He made it clear that the United States was prepared to launch a strike against the forces in Cuba and perhaps against the USSR if the forces were not removed. Because the United States had both overall nuclear predominance and nonnuclear superiority in an area of vital importance to it—the Caribbean—the Russian leaders believed the American threat and withdrew their missiles and aircraft.

In reaction to this public demonstration of their weakness, however, the Soviet leaders began a new program of strategic armament with development and, ultimately, deployment of a whole new line of missiles. This effort showed up in a steadily rising level of Soviet miltary expenditure beginning after 1965.

1967– : The Period of Essential Equivalence

From 1966 until 1975, the United States was deeply involved in another long, painful, and costly land war in Asia, this time in Vietnam. The effort, which finally failed, was to prevent North Vietnam–supported Communist guerrillas from taking over the government of South Vietnam. During the war, American military expenditures climbed to new heights. But by the time of gradual American withdrawal, public disgust with the war and with some of the excesses of the cold war produced a broadly based desire to cut the military budget. As a result, by 1973 American military expenditure had dropped below the pre-Vietnam level, remaining there until 1976, when it resumed a slow climb.

Meanwhile, the Soviet Union maintained its military buildup in conventional as well as nuclear arms. Since about 1972, it has matched or outspent the United States and has effectively caught up to the United States in strategic nuclear forces. While there remains some substantial controversy over the precise nature of

the Soviet–American strategic balance during most of this period, the majority of observers characterize it as one of "essential
equivalence," more or less a situation of parity when all elements of strategic weapons are taken into account.

True, there has been some controversy over whether the United
States has actually fallen behind in the strategic arms race. President Reagan fed these fears in an April 1982 news conference
in which he claimed, "On balance the Soviet Union does have
a definite margin of superiority." The President's assertion,
however, was immediately challenged, and not just by doves.
Senators Daniel P. Moynihan and Henry Jackson, long known
for their advocacy of greater military strength, denied that the
USSR was ahead. So did the (Republican) former Secretary of
Defense, James Schlesinger. Just a month before, the Joint Chiefs
of Staff, in their annual military posture statement, had said,
"A major attack on the United States or its allies would result
unquestionably in catastrophic retaliatory damage to the Soviet
Union." And the morning following the President's statement,
Richard Burt, director of the Bureau of Politico–Military Affairs
of the State Department, was compelled to explain on CBS news:
"What the President actually said was that the Soviets have the
momentum and we are worried about the trends."

Table 1-1 illustrates the essential facts about the changing strategic balance, with some projections to the situation in 1986 with
and without the limits provided for in the SALT II agreement.
You can see that at the beginning of 1963, the United States
maintained a clear numerical superiority in all classes of strategic delivery vehicles: ICBMs (land-based missiles such as Minuteman), SLBMs (submarine-launched missiles from vessels such
as the Polaris, Poseidon, and, in the 1980s, Trident submarines),
and long-range bombers (such as the B-52). Furthermore, in
most dimensions of quality (for instance, relatively undetectable
submarines and high-accuracy missiles) the United States also
was superior. By the 1970s, however, the Soviet effort had borne
fruit, and the USSR had caught up with, and eventually sur-
passed, the United States in numbers of ICBMs and SLBMs, but
not warheads. The Russians also went in for very large rockets
and warheads—equal to up to 25 megatons of chemical explo-

Table 1-1
Soviet and American Strategic Nuclear Forces, 1963–1986

	1963	1972	1981	1986 With SALT II	1986 Without SALT II
ICBMs					
United States	424	1054	1052	1052	1052
Soviet Union	90	1533	1398	1200	1604
MIRVed ICBMs					
United States	0	139	550	550	550
Soviet Union	0	0	652	820	1190
ICBM warheads					
United States	424	1332	2152	2152	2152
Soviet Union	90	1533	5354	6080	9110
SLBMs					
United States	224	656	576	640	712
Soviet Union	107	437	950	950	1016
MIRVed SLBMs					
United States	0	160	496	640	664
Soviet Union	0	0	192	380	444
SLBM warheads					
United States	224	2096	4656	6344	6584
Soviet Union	107	437	1334	2470	3740
Intercontinental bombers					
United States	630	457	348	348	348
Soviet Union	190	156	156	100	150
Strategic cruise missiles					
United States	0	0	0	2600	3400
Soviet Union	0	0	0	0	100
Total delivery vehicles					
United States	1278	2167	1975	4688	5512
Soviet Union	387	2110	2504	2250	2870
Total force loadings (warheads and bombs)					
United States	?	5598	9000	13,100	13,260
Soviet Union	?	2282	7000	8,750	13,150

Source: 1963 data from Bruce Russett and Bruce Blair, eds., *Progress in Arms Control? Readings from Scientific American* (San Francisco: W. H. Freeman and Company, 1979) pp. 6, 7; 1972–1986 data adapted from Herbert Scoville, Jr., *MX: Prescription for Disaster* (Cambridge: MIT Press, 1981), p. 67. All are originally derived from U.S. Department of Defense reports.

sive in some cases, in contrast to most American warheads of 1 megaton or less.

The apparent Soviet advantage in large warheads was not as important as it seemed, however, because a single large warhead is relatively inefficient compared with several smaller ones. Doubling a bomb's power increases its destructive capability only by about two-thirds. Instead of producing big missiles with single warheads, the United States concentrated on building missiles where each had Multiple (3 to 10) Independently targeted warheads or Reentry Vehicles (MIRVs) of high accuracy. These advantages in number of reentry vehicles and accuracy, coupled with the remaining American advantage in long-range bombers, basically compensated for Soviet advantages in size and number of missiles.

The result was a situation in which neither side could attack the other without knowing it would suffer enormous damage in the opponent's retaliation. According to Department of Defense (DOD) estimates, each side would have the ability to destroy at least one-third of the other's population and 60 percent of its industrial capacity in a strike. This gave both sides a "mutual assured destruction" (sometimes abbreviated as MAD) capability. It ensured that, for all intents and purposes, neither side could "win" a nuclear war.

Different aspects of this arrival at essential equivalence can be seen in Figure 1-3, which shows the strategic balance in terms of numbers of warheads, equivalent megatons (EMT), and hard-target kill (HTK) capability. Equivalent megatons is a widely used measure that takes into account the number of warheads and their explosive yield. Just as the United States is credited with an advantage in numbers of warheads (mostly because so many of its missiles are MIRVed), the USSR has an advantage in equivalent megatonnage because of its preference for very large warheads. Hard-target kill capability weights the equivalent megatonnage of each warhead by its accuracy. It shows an anticipated increasing Soviet advantage in the early 1980s as their new MIRVs come on-line, followed by substantial diminution of that advantage with deployment of new American systems. Important to the American position are the large-scale

16

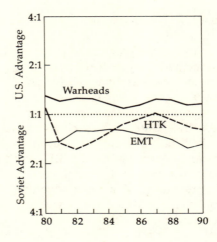

Figure 1-3
The Soviet–American strategic balance in the 1980s. [U.S. Department of Defense Authorization for Appropriations for Fiscal Year 1982, *Hearings Before the Committee on Armed Services of the United States Senate*, 97th Congress, 1st Session (Washington, D.C.: U.S. Government Printing Office, 1981), p. 144.]

deployment of new cruise missiles, a new force of Trident submarines and missiles, and the back-fitting of some older Poseidon subs with longer-range Trident missiles carrying eight large MIRVs each. The improvements to the SLBM force much more than make up for the retirement of a few old Polaris submarines with un-MIRVed missiles, which began in 1981.

Each of the different measures (warheads, EMT, HTK) addresses different aspects of the strategic balance and particular concerns about the relative advantage either side might have in a war or crisis. The projections into the late 1980s are tentative and depend on some assumptions about American and Soviet building programs that may not prove fully accurate. They are, nevertheless, fairly conservative assumptions from the American standpoint. By none of these measures does either side now, or in prospect, show a very substantial lead (all the ratios of advantage are well under two to one), and none would be likely to matter in any very practical way during the course of a nuclear war. Also, though the graph assumes deployment of the MX missile (under the old Carter administration plans), the improving American position in the mid eighties is not affected by it, since even the first MX missiles would not become operational until late 1986.

UPS AND DOWNS IN ARMS COMPETITION

Look again at the picture of overall military spending of the two superpowers presented in Figure 1-2. Expenditure levels, even allowing for the difficulties in discovering and valuing Soviet expenditures, are only a very imperfect way to measure military effort or capability. For one thing, they include all sorts of expenditures—for conventional (nonnuclear) forces, such as surface ships and armored vehicles, as well as for strategic nuclear arms, and for troops' payrolls as well as for weapons. The totals are compiled once a year (with the annual budgetary cycle), although a more frequent evaluation might better reflect a response to immediate international tensions.

Expenditure totals lag greatly behind civilian and military decisions to acquire weapons. For instance, in the U.S. political system, the process begins when the military services request a certain level of expenditure. Their request is then approved or modified by the Joint Chiefs of Staff and the Secretary of Defense and then is approved or modified again by the White House and the Office of Management and Budget. The expenditure must then be authorized by Congress. After that, still another procedure, managed by a different set of congressional committees, is necessary to appropriate the funds. Only then can the funds be spent. Of course, with buying something as complex and expensive as a modern strategic weapons system, it is usually several years before all the funds can be spent to produce a finished weapon. Thus a long time goes by between some international event that may lead to an upsurge of military spending and the actual expenditure of large sums. Furthermore, strategic arms represent only a small fraction (about 10 percent) of the typical military budget. These factors make it difficult, but not necessarily impossible, to see any connection between what one country does and what another does.

Also, in the real world, even superpowers react not just to each others' moves but to the acts of other states as well. For instance, the Soviet Union clearly is worried about China as well as about the United States. For the past 20 years it has maintained about 50 modern divisions on its frontier with China, and about 20 percent of all Soviet military spending is directed toward the Chinese threat. As for the United States, the big burst of spending during the late 1960s was due to its involvement in Vietnam, not to any sense of direct menace from the USSR.

Despite all this, some patterns do emerge from looking at this graph in the context of other knowledge about the international situation. First, you can clearly see the upsurge in American military spending with the onset of the Korean War. At the beginning, those expenditures were mainly just to fight the war itself, but they very soon turned into a much broader rearmament. Second, there is a much smaller but still discernible upsurge in American spending shortly after 1960—a response to *Sputnik* and the alleged missile gap. At about the same time as both of these American upsurges, the Soviet Union also raised its spending, though by lesser amounts. Later, you can see a steady rise in Soviet spending beginning after 1965 but probably, at least in part, reflecting decisions taken after the Cuban missile crisis. This increase has been maintained ever since, despite the Americans' restraint after the end of the Vietnam War. Finally, you can see a renewed American effort beginning in 1976 and continuing to the present.

This continuing and often parallel increase by both powers since the mid seventies is what some people mean by the term *arms race*—an image of the two superpowers racing against each other and reacting to each other's exertions in an upward spiral. The term is a slippery one when applied to the long history of Soviet–American superpower relations, however, because the upward trend is not always in evidence for the United States.

ASPECTS OF THE ARMS RACE

In the next chapter, we shall look more intently at where the nuclear arms race has brought us: We shall examine the present balance of forces, the efforts to build the kinds of weapons that would discourage attack, and the continuing fear that something will happen to upset the mutual balance of terror that remains the basic deterrent to nuclear war. Chapters 3 and 4 will be devoted to some underlying questions about the arms race. First, how dangerous or costly is it really? We must be alert not just to the wasted resources spent on arms but to the risk that the arms race, rather than deterring war, makes war more likely, and to the increased level of damage that would surely result from a war of nuclear states armed to the teeth. Following that, we shall consider a variety of explanations of why arms races—and this one in particular—occur. These explanations include both views that arms build-ups are responses to other states' arming and aggressive acts and views that arms purchases are primarily a result of purely internal economic, political, and bureaucratic interests. Both kinds of views show an important aspect of the truth.

Chapter 5 considers other aspects of the arms race as a response to another state's acts, especially the way in which one state's actions can provoke another's, with the second state in turn provoking the first in an ever-upward deadly spiral. Chapter 6 extends this perspective from arms purchases to political and military acts in crisis. Political crises are almost unavoidable in Soviet–American relations. Severe political crises stemming from conflicts of interest—in Europe, Asia, or the Middle East—threaten to be the most militarily dangerous periods, as each state tries to act tough and convince the other that it is willing to risk war to protect important national positions. It is in such crises, not in times of normal "peaceful" relations, that the threat of nuclear war becomes real.

One response to the wish to defend many different kinds of "national interests" with nuclear weapons has been the development of theories of limited nuclear war. Chapter 7 considers those theories as well as other efforts to restrain the horrors of actually fighting wars with large-scale weapons of mass destruction. These efforts deserve careful and critical scrutiny. They reveal how deeply the strategy and tactics of modern warfare are interwoven with central moral and ethical issues that should not be ignored. Finally, in the last chapter we shall review various efforts to negotiate agreements for arms control and disarmament. Some of these efforts occurred earlier in history, with simpler weapons; others have been addressed, with mixed success, to modern nuclear weapons. We conclude with some lessons from that experience and with a real but still precarious hope for the future.

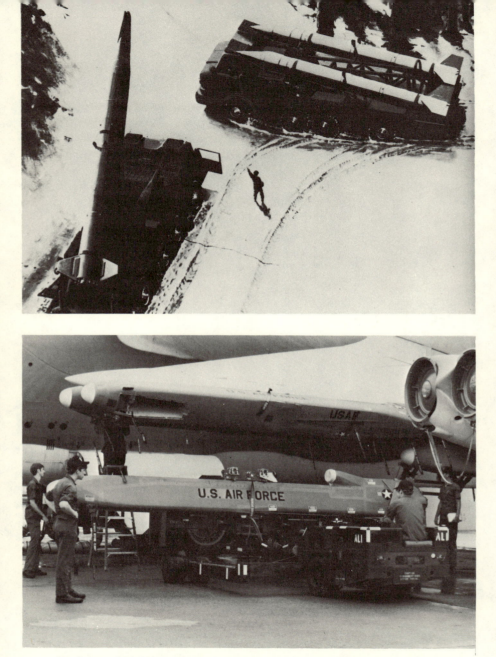

Top: Soviet "FROG" tactical missiles and launchers. *Bottom:* Boeing Air Launched Cruise Missile (ALCM) being mounted on the wing of a B-52 bomber. (Courtesy of U.S. Air Force, released by Department of Defense.)